INTRODUCTI
Welcome to JumpStart M‹

M000251632

Matthew 28:18-20 (NLT)
Jesus came and told his disciples,
"I have been given all authority in heaven and on earth.
Therefore, go and make disciples of all the nations,
baptizing them in the name of the Father and the Son
and the Holy Spirit. Teach these new disciples
to obey all the commands I have given you. And be sure of this:
I am with you always, even to the end of the age."
Jesus

2 Timothy 2:2 (NLT)
You have heard me teach things that have been confirmed
by many reliable witnesses. Now teach these truths to other trustworthy
people who will be able to pass them on to others.

Jesus called us to make disciples and St. Paul obeyed. That is the short, sweet, one sentence justification for the book you hold in your hand. Jesus Christ, our Lord Savior and God told us to make disciples. Why do churches and ministries give so much time and money to everything else? It's time to trust Jesus and do what He said, how He said to do it.

In the city of Abidjan on the Ivory Coast of Africa I stood in a sun-drenched field with 35,000 Africans who had traveled hours, even days to stand in the sun and worship Jesus without shade or seats. In America Sunday church attendance plummets if there is a cloud in the sky daring to suggest a drop of rain. To many believer's trifle with Jesus instead of following Him wholeheartedly. He is part of their life, but not the foundation. He is in the car, but not driving. One on one discipleship has the power to change that.

If the parable of the sower were told today Jesus would say believers are getting eaten by birds, dying without roots, and choked out by the cares of this world. Over the past thirty years of pastoral ministry I have seen to many abandon the race and too few explode with 30, 60, and 100-fold growth. I wrote JumpStart Volumes One and Two to give Christian leaders a working model for birthing a disciple making process in their ministry setting. JumpStart Mentor Training is the companion volume intended to guide you through the process of recruiting, training, and leading self-replicating disciple making mentors! It might sound scary right now. But Jesus told us to do this. If we will humbly obey the Lord's call to make disciples I believe He will keep His promise to build His church.

THE PURPOSE OF JUMPSTART
FROM PAUL'S DOCTORAL PROJECT PROPOSAL.
WRITTEN IN 2013

The purpose of this project is to train seven mentors in the use of JumpStart. The potential of this project is disproportionate to the seeming simplicity of the purpose statement for several important reasons.

First, NorthPoint [The church I pastored.] has been developing their Life Group format for the past five years. A design team has been working on focusing the Celebration service for the past year. It is time to develop the Mentoring dimension of our ministry model. The congregation has heard about JumpStart and people are excited to see the training process begin.

Second, the first seven mentors are the beginning of a cycle designed for reproduction. The recruiting and training of the mentors presupposes their intention to recruit and train others. The goal is an open-ended multi-generational expanding system.

Third, there is a synergy between *oikos* evangelism and JumpStart. As people express an interest in knowing Jesus, or growing in their faith, leaders will endeavor to connect them with a JumpStart trained mentor. Training mentors with a diversity of ethnicity, age, gender, and interests will allow greater flexibility in connecting a seeker, or growing believer, with the most compatible mentor possible.

Fourth, NorthPoint has the goal of raising up additional Shepherds with the ability to lead a Life Group. JumpStart will be the first step in that training process. When the Shepherd of a Life Group recognizes leadership potential in a group member, they can utilize JumpStart as the means of establishing a sixteen-week spiritual conversation based upon key Biblical topics. JumpStart facilitates conversation in the areas of Celebration, Life Groups, Mentoring, Shepherding, spiritual life and leadership within the Body of Christ.

Fifth, people beyond NorthPoint have expressed an interest in using JumpStart for mentoring. It would not be difficult to reformat the material presented in this project for usage in a more time-intensive manner. This training model would facilitate the possibility of flying to a distant location and training potential mentors preselected by their church leaders who had worked through several sessions in preparation for the training.

[As I write this in 2016 NorthPoint has trained dozens of mentors willing and able to disciple new members of the church. There are currently multiple new believers experiencing mentoring. It is now time to begin point five above, and share this process with other churches and ministries.]

Part One:
What is JumpStart and how do I use it?

In Part One we will examine the nuts and bolts of JumpStart. I will guide you through the process of selecting your first generation of mentors. We will discuss who to choose, and why. I will give you application forms in the appendix you can use with your candidates.

I will guide you through each part of the Sessions. There is more going on "Under the hood," than meets the eye. JumpStart is perfect for the missionary looking for a "Church in a Box" to leave with an indigenous pastor. Or for a campus pastor to use with a college student. Volume one can be a new believers class and volume two your ministry leader training track. Session sixteen can be used to build a Biblical triangle consisting of Celebration, Life Groups, and Mentoring with the word of God and prayer on the inside, and OIKOS relational evangelism on the outside.

Through it all runs the principle of Relational Inductive Bible Study. We will explore how two or three believers, God, and their Bibles can have an awesome time together. New believers in the church I pastored are learning to open the Scriptures, ask a question, and then bring out the answer for themselves. JumpStart will tool, or retool, the user in regards to their ability to hear and learn from God's written Word.

Part Two:
The Jethro/Moses Mentor Model

In Exodus 18 we see Jethro coming to visit his son in law Moses. You will examine every facet of that encounter and bring out modern day applications that are relevant in sports, medicine, law, military, business, and ministry. You will hear my stories and experiences as a mentor and a mentee. A mentee is the person on the receiving end of mentoring. You will read stories from my days in Special Forces, Glendale Police Department, PowerBurst, car sales, and multiple ministry settings.

Part Three:
The Biblical foundation for JumpStart.

In part three I cheat. I did a cut and paste from my Doctoral Project. It is the Theological Rationale for one on one or triad mentoring. It examines Moses and Jethro. Elijah and Elisha. Jesus with Peter, James, and John. And Paul with Timothy, Titus, and Silas. It is not exhaustive nor overly academic. It does look at some amazing Scriptures and principles from the Old and New Testament which cement the importance of mentor based discipleship in the plan of God through the ages.

JUMPSTART MENTOR TRAINING
AT YOUR CHURCH:

If you would like to schedule JumpStart
mentor training for your church or organization
please contact Pastor Paul.

Paul is also available for evangelism,
preaching, and small group training.

He Pastored NorthPoint Christian Fellowship
in San Bernardino, California for twenty-one years.

They survived and unified terrible division,
a name change, a change of constitution/by-laws,
$4,000,000 arson fire and sanctuary rebuild,
bankrupt insurance company, capital funds campaign,
six years of setup and teardown at an Elks Lodge.

Paul loves to coach Pastors and Churches who are in the midst
of trials, transitions, and visioning their next season of ministry.

He can be encouraging, thought provoking, and annoying.
Ex-Green Beret Pastors tend to think that way!

Call/Text:
1-909-855-9695

Email:
PAULMREINHARD@GMAIL.COM

Table of Contents

Part One:
What is JumpStart and how do I use it?

If you are a pastor, leader, or seeker wanting to learn
about Jesus you might wonder who the heck I am,
what JumpStart is, and why I think you should use it!
I would love to try and answer those questions.

Thought:

Take a minute before you begin reading and answer these questions. What is the discipleship need in your life, group, church, or ministry setting? What has God been speaking to your heart lately? What is your dream for a mentor ministry in you setting?

_____

_____

_____

_____

_____

_____

_____

_____

_____

_____

_____

_____

_____

_____

_____

_____

_____

FRONT LOAD

When I was doing my Doctor of Ministry degree at Golden Gate Seminary they used a great tool. They called it front loading. We did our reading and homework prior to arriving for our two-week intensive. It allowed us to maximize our time with the professors. We hit the ground running, ready to discuss the material. We could focus on application.

If you call me to your ministry site, I will follow this proven pattern. If your pastor or ministry leader conducts the training they can go longer but should cover these basic steps. Here is your essential front load. DO YOUR HOMEWORK, MAXIMIZE OUR TIME!

1. Read the Introduction box for each of the sixteen Sessions. This will give you an overview of where you are headed. You will see the flow before you go.

2. Read the OIKOS part of each Mentor Session. This will rap your mind around the outreach component of JumpStart. Reproduction is essential. Go deep and wide!

3. Read Part One of Mentor Training. This will introduce you to Relational Inductive Bible Study. It will define Relational, Inductive, and Bible Study. JumpStart is a unique blend of all three. It will also draw your attention to each of the "moving parts" of the JumpStart Session, and Mentoring. It will begin to unpackage the dynamic of using the Session, and the Mentoring. Each person should use it according to their gifts, personality, and their mentee's need.

4. Read Part Two of Mentor Training. Plug the Jethro/Moses Mentoring Model into your context. Draw principles that will help you "set the stage" for successful meetings with your mentee. Remember: You will not use every step every week. But there are important benchmarks that will help you connect with others.

5. On your own, work through Session Seven in Volume One and Session Eleven in Volume Two. Do the Session, and the Mentoring. Read the scriptures, answer the questions. This will give you the Biblical foundation for your call to be a mentor, and the Biblical foundation for disciple making.

6. I suggest pairing your first generation of trained mentors one with another. Since they have both read the Mentor Training, heard the discussion, and worked through two sample Sessions they should have a good grasp of where the process is heading. Then, I would have them begin at Session One and begin working through Volume One.

    As they work together they should be praying and speaking with the Mentor Training Team or pastor. Their focus should be inviting others into the Mentor process. There are two primary ways to purse this. First, when the first-generation mentors finish Volume One they can continue working with their partner through Volume Two, and begin Volume One with a new mentee.

Second, if they are not able to do two mentoring Sessions per week then finish Volume One and Two. After "graduation" begin the process with a new mentee.

Mentors need not always be working with two meetings at a time. This can become tiring and taxing on one's time and energy. However, it speeds up the getting started process. But, care should be taken that the emotional health, physical health, relational health, and time commitments of the mentor are of primary consideration. I would much rather see happy, healthy, committed people build something slow and strong. Angry, frustrated, burned out people either poison the well or quit. Remember: Moses spent forty years with Joshua and he turned out good.

7.   The first generation of mentors is essential for future success. Plants grow from the seed. So, chose well. Here are some characteristics of first generation mentors.

A.   In sync with the vision and the pastor and leaders of the church or ministry.

B.   Excited about growing in their personal faith.

C.   Open to sharing their faith with others. Or, open to learning how.

D.   Excited by the concept of mentoring another person. If they are scared, nervous, or see themselves as unable or unworthy, praise God. Humble teachable available people are perfect. If their heart is right the skills can be taught and the confidence imparted. Avoid the chronically toxic neurotic negative person. That is different than honest trepidation. First generation mentor training is not the place to fix your broken church members. Jesus picked functional disciples. Follow His example.

E.   Able to make a three hour per week commitment. One and one half hours is for homework and prayer. One and one half hours for meeting with their mentee.

F.   Avoid know it all's and control freaks. People who have been there, done that, and know everything are process killers. Mentors must not dominate, they must serve.

G.   Baby Christians with little or no theology need to be considered on a case by case basis. If they have proven to be faithful and teachable I might pair them with a healthy loving mature believer for their first-generation experience. If they "get it" they will be one of your most excited mentors. Pair them carefully. You are implanting powerful ministry DNA into a precious beautiful new believer. Do not waste them, or harm them. They might be your 30, 60, 100-fold mentor.

H.   I would make the sweeping statement that there is no wrong way to do JumpStart. Two or three willing well intentioned seekers, or believers with a Bible and JumpStart are liable to have their own amazing and unique experience.

Examples:

Two men in our church are my good friends and supporters of the ministry. They are 20 year veterans of the faith. It took them almost one year to do JumpStart. They met at Taco Bell with their study Bibles. The Sessions were just the starting point that sent them deeper into God's Word. Scott is about to begin mentoring a young man who was baptized this past Sunday. Frank is praying about going with me to India to train house church leaders. I am good with that.

A young lady, new to the church with no faith history is doing JumpStart with a mature woman of God. She is thrilled by what she is learning. The questions are leading her into the Biblical text and her mentor is helping her apply what she is learning to her life. She is getting baptized next Sunday and is helping lead our Celebrate Recovery. She told me she wants to mentor other women when she is ready. From Celebrate Recovery to JumpStart. I am thrilled.

This past Sunday a woman who is new to our church picked up JumpStart. She has a history of leading women's ministry in another setting. One of the senior saints of our church saw her with JumpStart and asked me, "Does she have somebody to take her through it?" I said, "No." Marge said to me, "I will talk to her Wednesday night when we are together." Marge is one of my trusted senior saints who has worked through JumpStart. If she does JumpStart with the new lady, and gives me a thumbs up, then I know we can release the new lady to do ministry here at NorthPoint because she has studied our DNA, and Marge has had sixteen weeks to build a relationship and vet her theology. Call it doing my pastoral relational due diligence. It is a win-win situation.

I.   I would not suggest putting the church grump into your first generation of JumpStart Mentors. You want open and excited spirits who will engage with open minds. See your first generation as the seed. Get the best you can with the greatest potential for growth and reproduction, then water them well.

8.   If I am called to your church to help train first generation mentors we will begin with an overview of the JumpStart mentor based disciple making method. Because you have frontloaded the material we can jump right in and discuss your questions, concerns, and goals for implementation. Then I will do Session Seven as a mentoring experience. I will be the mentor, and treat the group as the mentee. Then we will have lunch, followed by a discussion of the Jethro/Moses Mentoring Model. Our final training Session will be you, pairing with one or two others, and working through Session Eleven. We will conclude our day with a debrief of your experience, planning for implementation, and prayer! I would encourage pastors or ministry leaders to follow this pattern. If you are doing your own implementation of JumpStart I am available by phone to help any way I can. May God bless you!

Your Thoughts, Notes, and Questions:

What is JumpStart?
Chapter One

Let me begin by saying JumpStart is not another program for your ministry. It is not a Bible study. It is not a counseling course. It is not one more thing for the overcommitted members of your church to start doing. It is not fast. Let me say that again. It is not fast at all. If you have a denominational executive breathing down your neck looking for results I suggest Monday Night Football in the parsonage or a Pinterest Craft Fair. LOL

If you let us in, God might use JumpStart and I to shake up your church. It is also possible God will use it to begin a powerful, long lasting soul winning work of spiritual renewal in you and the people you serve. After forty years in the faith I am done playing games and wasting time. I have little or no patience with selfish people who think the church belongs to them. The church exists to train the found to find the lost. In the words of the Apostle, "I have become all things to all men that I may by all means save some." Anything less is sin and trifling.

I attended the Cell Church Symposium in Waco, Texas in June of 2009. Today it is October of 2016. Pastor Dion Robert from Abidjan, Ivory Coast, Africa stood in the pulpit and preached through his translator Jim Lassiter. He reached a point in his sermon where he authoritatively yet humbly commanded, "Go home and kill your church." His text was Galatians 2:19-20. His point was the people leading the church who are so alive to themselves that they are dead to the cause of Christ.

Galatians 2:19-20 (NLT)
For when I tried to keep the law, it condemned me.
So I died to the law—
I stopped trying to meet all its requirements—
so that I might live for God.
My old self has been crucified with Christ.
It is no longer I who live, but Christ lives in me.
So I live in this earthly body by trusting in the Son of God,
who loved me and gave himself for me.

I remember that sermon as if it were yesterday. Dead people don't care how long the sermon is, or how loud the music is, or what color the nursery is. Because dead people don't care. Dead people walk a day or two and stand in the hot sun for hours to hear the preaching of the gospel. Live people look out the window at the rain cloud, turn off the alarm, roll over and go back to sleep while their kids get up and watch cartoons. Live people disciple their children to be twice the sons and daughters of hell they are. Dead people do not. After eating and fellowshipping with Bill Beckham, Mario Vega, Robert Lay, Dion Robert, and Harold Weitsz I was freaking out. My soul was on fire.

I was walking to lunch with Ralph W. Neighbour, Jr. and thinking out loud about finding the right mentoring material for NorthPoint. Ralph looked at me intently and said, "Write one yourself." I was taken aback and asked, "Who am I to write a mentoring track?" Ralph looked into my eyes even more intently and said, "Why do you think I'm investing years of my life in you? So you can do nothing?" Ralph was mentoring me. He was coaching and challenging me. He was sowing vision into my heart and giving me the confidence and courage to chase a dream. That is what mentors do in the lives of mentees. Mentors take mentees to places they would never go by themselves.

For many months, I prayed, thought, and stewed about JumpStart. You can read about the day I finally sat to write at Georges Diner. It is in the preface of Volumes One and Two. Within the span of twenty minutes the outline took shape on a yellow legal pad with a blue ink pen. Over the next few years I preached it, wrote it, and eventually put it into vinyl three ring 8.5 x 11 binders. People at NorthPoint began to use it, and tell me all my mistakes. It took a while but I finally learned the finished product was more important than my ego. So now I can honestly say I appreciate people refining the questions, Biblical passages, or my grammar.

As people used it and I fixed it things worked better. In the fall of 2013 I was running the risk of timing out of my D. Min. I did not know what to do so once again I found myself face to face with Ralph. "You've come too far to quit," said he. "What do I do?" said I. Ralph looked across the table of the Cheese Cake Factory in Brea, CA. "Finish JumpStart and train mentors to use it." His son Ralph smiled encouragement. In July of 2014 I handed in my finished project. From Waco to the finished project was five years. From then until now, October 2016 was two more. My precious wife has watched me struggle, write, adjust, add, fix, and train mentors to utilize JumpStart over the past seven years.

Today, several years after I began beta testing JumpStart we have dozens of men and women who are currently working in, or have completed JumpStart. If you come to Christ at NorthPoint Christian Fellowship in San Bernardino, California there are people who would love to invest five months walking you through the sixteen progressive steps of JumpStart. They will help you drill down spiritual roots for a fruit bearing life in Christ.

When I began talking to NorthPoint about accountability, small groups, and mentoring people called us a cult. Pastoral colleagues asked denominational executives what I was doing to the church in San Bernardino. A wonderful young man we ordained went to pastor in a nearby city. The local ministerial association wondered if he was going to kill the church, the way I killed NorthPoint. Another young man I mentored worked in another church and was told he could begin small groups, but not like they did at NorthPoint.

Those were crazy transitional days. Today I am at a place of amazing joy as I prepare to step down from the Lead Pastor position I have held for the past twenty-one years. Last Sunday the church voted unanimously, by secret ballot, to call my 36-year-old son Chris to become their new Lead Pastor. He has been my partner in ministry over the past nine years and is ready to lead NorthPoint to her next level of ministry.

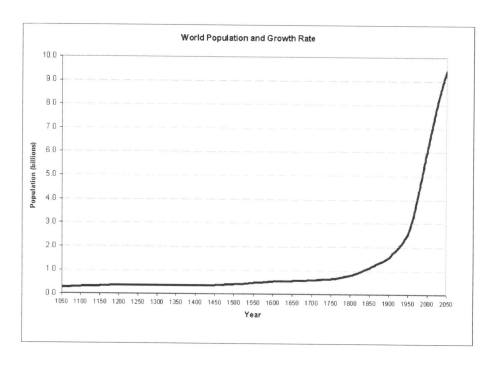

Last weekend I was at the Transformation Ministries Conference in Mesa, AZ. I had the pleasure and honor of hearing our Mission Lead, Dr. Willie Nolte, endorse both JumpStart and myself to our movement. He encouraged pastors and churches to connect and allow me to show them how to begin JumpStart in their ministry settings. What a journey! Patience and tenacious persistence is paying off.

Two weekends ago I attended the Group Life Conference with Nathan Neighbour and Mosaic Pomona, California. I stood at a book table and for the very first time sold and gave away copies of JumpStart. I talked with leaders about beginning a JumpStart mentor based discipleship process in their church. Little did they know that I was handing them a revolution in two short volumes. Seven years of prayer and work are being released.

It took the entire history of humanity to achieve one billion global population in the lifetime of my great grandfather. In my 61 years on the planet we have grown from 2.7 to 7.4

billion people.[1] If Jesus was serious about going into all the world and making disciples of all the nations then our potlucks and bingo will not get the job done. Jesus made disciples. It is slow, hard, and messy. But when the Spirit of God birthed a 3,000-member church in Acts 2 the leaders trained by Jesus were ready to run with the harvest. I want to see the church move from pedantic addition to explosive multiplication. Discipleship is the key. JumpStart is just one of the tools available. But if it is right for you, I would love to help you use it fully, to the glory of God! Amen.

To the artists and doodlers among us I bring greetings.
Use this space to draw what God is stirring in your heart right now.
As you sketch your way through JumpStart consider
scanning and texting/emailing me your visual thoughts.
I would love to see them!

---

[1] Geohive.com

9

How do I use it?
Chapter Two

In this chapter, we will examine each part of a JumpStart Session, or Mentoring. I will identify the various boxes, words, and titles. There are more moving parts to JumpStart than first meets the eye. There are prayers, thoughts, remembers, verses to study, and memorize. The OIKOS track is of special importance. After each number below there is a brief teaching, an example, and lines for your thoughts and questions. If I come to your ministry site to do training I will begin here, and focus on your questions, thoughts, concerns, and observations. So write them down while they are fresh in hour mind. If your pastor or church leader is doing a training I encourage you to follow the Q & A format. If you are reading this for yourself, it is still valuable to make notes you can come back to in the future. Who knows, maybe you are Mentor Trainor God is raising up!

ONE:

Every Session of JumpStart will begin with a text box that gives a brief Introduction to that Session. I like to know where I am headed before I begin a journey. Reading this box at the beginning of a mentoring Session can re-orient you to the week's Lesson. Be sure and read all sixteen boxes before training day. It will give you a good overview.

Introduction:

I heard a joke about football and church being very much alike. Because, on Sunday people who need exercise sit in the seats and watch tired people who need a rest! The awesome truth is God has work for each of His children to do. Church is not about the rested saints watching the exhausted leaders run around. The true church is all about leaders, called and equipped by God, raising up, training, and releasing an army of disciples! All of God's people are invited! How awesome! You have an important part to play in the Body of Christ.

_____

_____

_____

_____

_____

TWO:

The Introduction box is followed by a Key Verse. This verse attempts to capture the essence of the Lesson. I would suggest writing the verses on a three by five card. Then punch a hole in the corner of the stack of cards and tie, loop, or ring them together. If you write the book, chapter, and verse on the back you have a homemade scripture memory pack. The sixteen short verses will give you a great mental index of the topics you covered.

Key Verses for Memorization and Reflection: Ephesians 2:10 (NLT)
For we are God's masterpiece. [KJV: His Workmanship]
He has created us anew in Christ Jesus,
so we can do the good things he planned for us long ago.

_____

_____

_____

THREE:

The Lesson heading will lead deep into the topic. It expands upon the Introduction. They will tend to be longer, although in this case they are roughly the same. You can see it as more information to prepare you for your journey into the Word.

Lesson:

All too often, the church appears to be a place where people go to watch the show! The place where sinful people sit in the seats and watch the holy professional lay the smack down! Nothing is farther from the truth. God has uniquely gifted and called every one of His precious children into service. Next week we will look at the wonderful diversity of spiritual gifts at work within the Body of Christ. Today we are going to focus on every believer's call! Allow God's Word, not church tradition, to define your place in the Body.

_____

_____

_____

FOUR:

Every Lesson will include Scriptures from the Old and/or New Testament. I chose the New Living Translation 2nd Edition. This was done to accommodate the greatest span of reading levels while maintaining evangelical integrity. You will find some questions have just the right amount of fill in the blanks if you use the NLT. Feel free to use your NKJV,

ESV, NASB, NIV or other favorite translation. Just remember that if I send you into a verse to find three specific things, another translation might have 2 or 4. It does not make them wrong, just impacted by the translation committee's choice of words. You will see later that Session four on the Holy Ghost is based off the NASB. I will explain why later.

1.   Check out Mark 1:16-20.

A.   What call did Jesus give to the disciples?

_____

_____

_____

_____

FIVE:

Every so often you will see the word, Reflection. This indicates I had a thought, story, or just wanted to "share." These may contain my opinions regarding the workings of a church, or other observations about life and ministry. I would like to believe my view of Scripture, church, and life are always right. Sadly, that is just not true. Just ask my precious wife of thirty-eight years. She will be happy to tell you.

Let me be clear and honest. Any time you see the word Reflection, you are entering the realm of my personal teaching and opinion. It is not Scripture; it is not God breathed. I would like to believe it might be useful to you. I would like to believe after forty years of walking with Jesus my observations have some basis in fact. But never allow my words to be the basis for dissention in your mentoring relationship, small group, or church. If you are going to draw lines and lock horns, do it over the written Word of God. That is worth circling the wagons over. Never pit my view of the church against the leaders God has placed in authority over the ministry you are part of. If at some point you find them opposing the clear and prevalent teaching of Scripture, that is worth a conversation.

Reflection:

Many churches follow a traditional manmade pattern for ministry. A man or a woman goes off to school and "Learns to be a minister." When that person graduates, they return to the local church where they spend their life "Doing the ministry." The paid professional is so good at doing the ministry they can gather a faithful flock of tithing followers. Over time a splendid co-dependent relationship develops. The pastor loves being the minister, and the people love receiving ministry. This ruins God's glorious plan for His church.

_____

_____

_____

SIX:

A Thought might have a little more weight than a Reflection. A thought is an observation about the text, or something I strongly believe to be true. Again, I encourage you to save your stubborn moments for the written Word. But you might want to give me the benefit of the doubt on my Thoughts. Take the time to discern what I am saying, and why, before you just blow it off. In fact, call me, text me, or email me. I love to discuss what I have written. And if you convince me, I will change it. Iron does sharpen iron!

Thought:

Moses was not worried about his ego or position. He wanted the people of God to receive all God had for them. He was secure enough in himself not to care who God used. Moses cried out with the heart of a true leader. He wanted God's spirit for all of God's people. He wanted God to use all of them to His glory. Moses prayer came true on the day of Pentecost, fulfilling the prophecy of Joel.

SEVEN:

Each Session ends with a Conclusion. This is the preacher in me summing up, wrapping up, tying up the loose ends. It is me throwing something at you one more time. If it is in the conclusion it is important. If it is in the Conclusion, it is a core thought to the Lesson. I would encourage mentors to digest the Introduction, Memory Verse, Lesson, and Conclusion. The Scriptures might wander around a bit. I may pull in different trains of thought. But the Introduction, Memory Verse, Lesson, and Conclusion will give you a clear overview of the Session. This can be helpful for people who tend to wander. It does not hurt to know the theme of the week, and attempt to stay with it. Now, having said that. If the Spirit of God is working or speaking in a specific area feel free to land there. If God is leading, go ahead and chase the bunny. If your mentee is just a random, unfocused type then use the theme to pull them back and keep them on track. Within three Sessions you will know what you need to do. Follow the Spirit, or get back on track.

Conclusion:

It is important for believers to grow in ministry faith and skill. Christians should be lifelong learners. However, the Lord did not call us to serve because of our skill and knowledge. Christ called us out of darkness into the light by His grace. The Holy Spirit gave us gifts to use in service to the world, and the church. God gave us the role of priests in the house of Christ. Everything we have comes by the grace of God. The great truth is God has called, gifted, and placed each of His children in the Body of Christ according to His good purpose. When each of us does our work under the blessing and anointing of Christ the church grows and prospers. It is an awesome plan.

_____

_____

_____

EIGHT:

If you hit Remember you have encountered preaching. It is me wanting to drill something into the heart of your mentee. It is important, it is encouraging, it is a teaching moment, or it is a testimony. It is me wanting to turn the screw a couple more revolutions. It is me wanting to be sure you get it. It is me not wanting to let go. It is me doing what I am doing with you right now! In the words of my father, it is me, "Not knowing when to leave well enough alone!" [Remember box is on the next page.]

Doodle Space:

REMEMBER:

We try, we fail, we learn,
and hopefully do better next time!

My dad taught me to ski
when I was five years old.
He told me repeatedly,
"If you are not falling, you are not trying!"

The important thing is to keep trying.
Get back up when you fall down.
Keep learning, keep serving!
Someday you will get it right,
or at least get better.

The glory does not belong to you anyway!

God will take your best efforts,
touch them with His power and glory,
and use them to accomplish amazing things!

You are a valuable and precious member
of the living Body of Jesus Christ.

Never allow any person to keep you from doing what
God has called and gifted you to do!

NINE:

Fasten your seat belt because you have come to the schizophrenic part of JumpStart. This will be one of the most liberating and/or frustrating parts of JumpStart. It all depends on your personality, training, experience, and approach to written material. I have taught the Bible or mentored over forty years. Truthfully, I can make it up as I go along. That is not bad for someone with A-D-D. I can end up in some great places. I see Scripture in my head, and the flow of the passage unlocks.

Years ago, a theology student from Azusa Pacific University visited NorthPoint when I was preaching. After the message, he came up to me and said, "You are doing form critical analysis in an exegetical format and nobody knows it." I laughed. Only theology majors say things like that. I just tell old stories and pick out the good parts.

So, let me apply this. When I do JumpStart, I walk my mentee through the Session scripture by scripture and box by box. I know the material, the mentee, and God. I let the Spirit guide where the conversation goes. I will often have my mentee do the Session and put a check mark by the questions, prayers, boxes, reflections, or anything else that spoke to them. Then we will journey page by page and I will ask, "So, where did God connect with you?" I let them lead me to the spots they want to go. If I sense them avoiding an area within a Session I will follow the Spirit in, as He leads and the mentee allows.

As I was first writing JumpStart my son kept reminding me I have counseled and taught the Bible for a living. I was working on my third degree. Chris said, "You better give people some questions to use. Help them out. Show them how to go beyond or into the Biblical text. Help them connect relationally with people." I went back through JumpStart and added the mentoring section. That is the source of your problem if you are a detail person like my wife. She wants to know what to do. She wants clear marching orders.

Do I use the Session?
Do I use the mentoring?
Do I do one, or the other, or both?
My answer does not help her, "YES!"

A very well educated pastor in my cluster who is looking at JumpStart asked exactly how the Session and the Mentoring worked. I said, "YES!" He was about as impressed as my wife. He suggested I merge the Session and the Mentoring into one new thing. I told him I do not have the time, and I'm not exactly sure how to do it.

So here is the schizophrenic reality. JumpStart has a Session/Lesson section, and it has a Mentoring section. I want you to use them in whatever manner works for you. If you can apply the Bible in a relational way you may have limited use for the mentoring section. If you are a great counselor, listener, touchy/feely people person you may need to track deeper into the Biblical material in the Lesson. I honestly use it all. But I have used it enough times that I know the questions, and areas of focus in the Mentoring section so I can pull them in as needed with my mentee.

In the latest re-written edition, I have added stories, zingers, landmines, and ambushes. People who have used JumpStart in the past need to re-read the boxes. There are things for people who struggle with God because of negative father issues. There is a box for pastors and leaders unwilling or unable to release control and allow their church to join this millennium. There is a re-write in the close of Session eight that leads into a much more missional evaluation and application of our spiritual gifts. So even JumpStart veterans need to read the mentoring sections and become familiar with the fishing poles, bait, and lures I have put there for them. Remember: Christianity is a contact sport!

Jumpstart Mentoring 7

"The Invitation"

_____

_____

_____

TEN:

Conversation Starters exist to help you connect. JumpStart is, and is not a Bible study. I can read Scriptures on love, exegete them properly, and give the right Sunday School answers while hating your guts. I can have my arms folded, my eyes averted, my legs crossed, and my car keys in my hand; jiggling them loudly while you sing "Jesus loves me this I know" and it won't do me any good. The mentoring time is for application, and emotional interaction, not just intellectual and cognitive repartee. There is nothing more frustrating than Biblical correctness without emotional engagement and ownership. There is a classic story about the time when Professor Tony Campolo was speaking to a church crowd and not getting his point across. He finally looked at them and said, "It is _ _ _ _ _ _ _ _ that children all around the world die of malnutrition every day. And the sad thing is your more upset about the word I used than the dying children."

The point of the Conversation Starter is to start a conversation. It is designed to get you out of some Biblical passage and into today's world. You will read more about this in the Second Level Question section of the next chapter. We need to engage God with our body, mind, and soul. Not just quote Bible answers like robots. Information without obedience is intellectual idolatry.

Sadly, years ago I sat through a review panel of pastor's children, most of whom were not walking with Jesus. The bottom line for these teenagers was the hypocrisy their ministry parents practiced. They were brilliant theologians on Sunday, and idiots at home. It is not enough that we "Know the Word." We must also live and practice the word.

Conversation Starters:

1.   Think about past church experiences you have had. Have you been an involved participant or a passive spectator?

_____

_____

_____

_____

ELEVEN:

Near the end of each mentoring section there is an OIKOS section. This is critical, and not to be missed. I have re-written the OIKOS section in this edition. Over the span of 16 Sessions the OIKOS theme will develop. It will lead you to think of your OIKOS, or circle of influence. These are the 8-15 people God has strategically placed in your life. Over the weeks you will begin loving, then praying, and then serving your OIKOS. You will practice writing your testimony and pray for an opportunity to share it with your OIKOS. You will work on how to invite your OIKOS to your baptism. OIKOS is the outreach arm of JumpStart. Discipleship without outreach is unbalanced. The goal of JumpStart is to raise up SOUL WINNING DISCIPLE MAKING CHRIST FOLLOWERS. I will consider you a JumpStart success story when the mentee your mentee mentored has a mentee. At its core JumpStart is designed to be self-replicating. If JumpStart ends up sitting on your shelf with all the other books you have read I will feel like I failed.

I am going to confess my three-secret objectives hidden inside JumpStart. Here they are. First, I want you to know how to read the Bible for yourself and pull out truths that are relevant to your life. Then I want you to apply them, live them, and do them. I want the written Word to come alive in your day to day life. Second, I want you to know how to lead another person to Christ, disciple them, and infect them with a passion to share Christ with their OIKOS. Third, but not least, in Session sixteen I want you to get infected with the Biblical basis for Celebration size groups, Small Groups, and One-on-One or Triad Mentoring. Don't let my secret escape. But JumpStart contains the DNA for a worshiping Church, built one Disciple at a time, Gathered into Groups, and fully functioning as the Body of Christ. One, Two, and Training are a trilogy designed to incite spiritual revolution.

I would suggest for all Mentors to read the sixteen OIKOS sections in order, in one sitting. Get the flow. Understand what I am after. Then lead your mentee down the path to soul winning one safe and easy step at a time. Don't scare them. Let them discover. As you do so expect the Holy Spirit to show up and do things way beyond your control.

OIKOS:

As you begin to see yourself as a servant of God I pray He opens your eyes to the mission field around you. One of the most powerful tools for impacting the world is service. I may not agree with your theology but I will probably accept a cup of cold water on a hot day. We are living in a world where people can be afraid of one another. You know God has already given you a special circle of influence to serve. Last week you began praying for your OIKOS. This week I challenge you to begin looking for ways to serve your OIKOS. I pray your OIKOS has noticed the change in your spirit. I pray they attend your baptism. I pray they are sensing God working in their lives because of your influence. And now I pray God allows you to love on your OIKOS through service and good deeds.

_____

_____

_____

TWELVE:

Each mentoring section has a Closing Reflection. You might call this the benediction of the Session. It is a final cheer for you, your mentee, and what God is doing. It is where my gift of WOO, or encouragement, gets to slip out. I am for you. God is for you. We both love you. I want you to hear it, get it, own it, and live it. I want you to succeed in spiritual ways you have never succeeded in before. I want to close the mentoring section with an affectionate kick in the butt. Go, fly, and soar. Do and be what God already knows you are! DO YOU HAVE IT MENTOR? YOU CAN DO THIS. THE GATES OF HELL CAN'T CONTAIN WHAT GOD IS RELEASING IN YOUR MENTEE THROUGH YOU. YOU ARE STARTING A DISCIPLE MAKING PYRAMID WITHOUT END!

Closing Reflection:

Nike says "Just Do It."

Uncle Sam says, "I Want You!"

Jesus says, "If you will follow Me I will make you a fisher of men." He has called you, saved you, gifted you, and placed you in His Body the Church. He desires you to trust Him, and use the gifts He has given you. More than anything else, Jesus is asking you to be faithful! If you will be faithful and willing, God will use you to His glory! Do the best you can do, with what you have, where you are, and leave the rest to God!

_____

_____

THIRTEEN:

You will also find random prayers every so often. My written prayers are no better or worse than your prayers. I have no magic pastoral powers. I am for extemporaneous prayers. I am for Holy Ghost prayers. I am for written prayers. I am for prayer. If my prayers can serve as a guide and motivation, enjoy them. Just never be tied down or limited by them. They are there to lift you up, encourage you, and set you free!

VOLUME ONE BENEDICTION:

Lord God Almighty.
I receive Jesus Christ of Nazareth as my Lord and Savior.
I accept You as my Heavenly Father.
I invite the Holy Spirit to come into my life,
and be my teacher, guide, director, and comforter.

I submit my body, mind, soul, and resources to Christ
and His Kingdom. Lead me, guide me, direct me,
and protect me. I want to go where you want me to go,
say what you want me to say, do what you want me to do,
and be the man or woman of God you have called me to be.

Deliver me from the evil powers of this age.
Use me to your glory and receive me
into your eternal heavenly Kingdom when
my earthly journey in this world is finished.

In the mighty name of Jesus Christ,
AMEN

Is there a special thought that is running around your mind right now? How can you see God using you, and JumpStart?

Hello art friends. I pray your visual hearts and minds
are exploding with ideas about using JumpStart.
This is your space!

RELATIONAL INDUCTIVE BIBLE STUDY
FOR JUMPSTART MENTORING
Chapter Three

God's Word is at the very heart of JumpStart Mentoring. When two or three people gather in the name of Jesus He promised to be with them. The Holy Spirit is the ultimate teacher of the written Word. Our desire is for a mentor and a mentee to open their hearts and minds to what God has for them in His Word. The Scriptures you will study and the mentor questions you will explore exist to help you in that process.

The word RELATIONAL tells us this process is about people. It is not only about personal Bible study. It is about studying, exploring, and experiencing the Bible with another person. The word INDUCTIVE tells us we are going to begin with the Biblical text, and allow it to speak to us. Mentor and mentee will open the Word of God together and allow it to speak into their lives. Then, together, the mentor and mentee will explore how to apply what God is teaching them.

These questions will guide the mentor and mentee in their exploration of the Scriptures. These questions are not the ending. They are only the beginning. They are a starting point, from which to begin exploring, understanding, and applying the Scriptures.

Each session of JumpStart will begin with homework. The mentor and mentee will individually read the Session and answer the various questions. Some of these questions will take you directly to the Scriptures. Others will explore your thinking, feelings, and life experiences. Use the following questions to assist you in reading, understanding, and applying the Word of God to your life. Remember: JumpStart is not the only way. It is a way. But if you trust it, and don't fight it, it will guide you through a wonderful path filled with life changing Scriptures. I have seen it work many times already. Over the span of sixteen Session you will be amazed where the Word and Spirit allow you to go.

PREPARATION:

1.   The New Living Translation 2nd Edition is the text used for most Bible based questions. Session 4, *The Power* uses the New American Standard Bible. If you use another translation, be aware that certain questions might not perfectly align with the word choices of your chosen translation. If you use another translation, have a copy of the NLT on hand to help clarify the intent of a given question if needed.

2.   Begin your personal time in the Word, and your time together with your mentee, with prayer. Ask God to forgive your sins, and clear your mind. Ask Him to lead you into His Word. Ask Him to send the Holy Spirit to be your guide. Be open to what He wants to show you. As you get to know your mentee you will recognize when God is stirring.

INDUCTIVE QUESTIONS:

1.   What does the Biblical text say?

Read the verse or the passage as you would read any book or newspaper. What are the simplest and most evident points of the passage? If the text says, "Jesus wept" then the simplest point of the passage is that Jesus was weeping.

2.   What did the text mean in its original context?

Every text has a context. If you hand me a ladder in a grocery store so I can get the green beans off the shelf it is profoundly different from you lowering a ladder into the well into which I have fallen. Both involve you, a ladder, and me. However, the emotion, the potential consequences, and the urgency are profoundly different. Look at the broader context of the text you are examining. Who is speaking? Who is the audience? Who else is listening? Where are they? Are they friends sitting in a boat fishing, or are they on trial for their life before a king and his council? Ask what the text meant in its cultural, geographic, and relational setting.

3.   What does the text mean today, in our culture and context?

The impact of culture on the intention and application of a Biblical text is a contested area of study. It is a topic beyond the scope of this training. It is still important that we find a way to build a bridge from what the Bible meant there to them, and what it means hear and now to us. Pastor Paul wrote JumpStart believing the God of the Bible desires to speak to us today through His written Word. A wise man once told him the Bible was like a fish, eat what you can, and leave the rest for later. Take the principles and teaching from Scripture and put them into practice in the most logical way possible.

4.   What is the text saying to you, now, in your present context?

When you believe that you understand what Scripture is saying, then God's expectation is for you to do it. Two important elements will serve to protect us in this process. First, is there a consistent theme in the Scriptures that supports what you believe God is telling you? Every major Biblical theme has numerous verses. Allow Scripture to support and confirm Scripture. Beware of building upon obscure verses. That is not to say God may not speak to you like that. God can do whatever He wants. However, if you think He is, see the next element.

Second, do theology in community. Talk to your Pastor, Shepherd, Coach, or Christian friends about what you think God is saying to you in His Word. Read several respected commentaries and find out what the historical interpretation and application of a text was. There is a lovely consistency to theology. The norm is for scholars of different seminaries, and different centuries to agree on the basic intention of most texts. There are a few topics where the church divides into camps. JumpStart has attempted to avoid these areas of division.

RELATIONAL APPLICATION:

1.   What is God asking me to be or do, or not be or do, in response to this text?

When you have a good grasp of what truth or principle the text is speaking in today's culture and context then apply it to your life. What do you need to do, not do, or be in response to what the Word is telling you?

2.   Is there anything keeping me from obeying this portion of God's Word?

This can be the toughest point of them all. What if there are things that complicate the seemingly simple act of obeying God? In some cultures, this can be life or death. In America, Jesus should affect your job, investments, relationships, marriage, kids, and friends. Choosing to obey what God has shown is the ultimate pivot point of your Christian faith. Obedience affects our relationship, which is the key to fruitfulness and joy in our walk with Jesus Christ. We can never lead another where we refuse to go.

3.   How can mentor and mentee help one another live according to the text?

This is where the relational mentoring, coaching, and disciple making aspects of JumpStart come into play. Trust, friendship, and a growing respect allow mentor and mentee to speak into one another's lives. Accountability is a healthy and integral part of the discipleship process. This is where discernment and experience play a crucial role. There is a fine balance between ministering, supporting, encouraging, and abusive prying. JumpStart is not a cult where we put people in a room and keep them awake for days on end until they break and embrace the point of view we want them to have.

JumpStart builds upon the premise that God calls people into discipleship relationships. These relationships must be rooted in love, grace, mercy, patience, kindness, and gentleness. Mentors should go as deep as a mentee is willing to go. Mentors must be ready for any conversation, confession, intervention, or occurrence. **The mentee is always the one who sets the pace. The mentee should never feel violated by a mentor.**

There may be times when the Spirit will call the mentor to linger, tarry, and remain on a question. Pastor Paul loves to ask people, "What is God saying to you?" If you see emotion, angst, or consternation [anxiety] upon the countenance [facial expression] of a mentee it is appropriate to ask them how the Scripture, question, or conversation is affecting them. Remember, the decision to share is always up to the other person. **We are partners, not pry bars!**

Allow the Word of God, and the Spirit of God, to do the work of God. Our job is to walk beside our mentee and help point them into whatever God has for them. As time goes on, your mentee should begin to encourage, teach, and challenge you just as much as you do them. Enjoy this sacred time God has given you to open His Word with another person. Trust that God will guide you into all the conversations He wants you to have. You do not need to force anything. Just follow the JumpStart process, and it will guide you into some amazing places! I pray the next few months are amazing for you!

What do the three key parts of JumpStart mean to you?

Relational:

_____

_____

_____

_____

_____

_____

_____

Inductive:

_____

_____

_____

_____

_____

_____

_____

Bible Study:

_____

_____

_____

_____

_____

_____

_____

Artist friends, what does it look like for a mentor,
a mentee, and God the Holy Spirit
to connect over a cup of coffee with an open Bible?

IMPLEMENTATION
Chapter Four

Thought: There was a method to my madness.
When I trained the first generation of mentors at NorthPoint to use JumpStart I used a backwards training process. Fist I led them through the process, then at our debrief and follow up training I told them what we did. The truth is I was probably making my plan up as went along, so I probably did not fully know where we were going in the beginning. It is always easier to draw the bullseye around the arrow you already shot into the barn.

JUMPSTART
MENTOR TRAINING
#1. What have we done?

_____

_____

_____

_____

_____

_____

BEGIN WITH PRAYER:

I prayed that God would send
just the right people
to participate in JumpStart.

Before anything was announced,
scheduled, or planned, I prayed!

GET ACQUAINTED:

We ate.
We prayed.
We previewed the sixteen sessions.
We agreed on a schedule.
We distributed material.
We explained the homework.

THE SETTING:

Meet in a place where you can talk.
Avoid kids, dogs, and spouses.
Food and beverages help break the ice.
Public places are good,
but pick a quiet corner,
away from walkways and kitchen.

THE FIRST MEETING:

Take time to connect.
Remember that the mentee does not
know what to expect.
Be very gentle.
Ask them how they are doing.
Take time to listen.
Do not rush into the lesson.

THE FIRST SESSION:

Work through the lesson line by line.
Use this time to discover your mentees
familiarity with the Word.
Sense their comfort level.
How much do they want to share?
Let them set the level!

MENTORING QUESTIONS:

Use the mentoring questions to explore the mentees spiritual history, and journey. Their family of origin holds many keys to their current understanding of God.

_____

_____

_____

_____

_____

_____

_____

_____

_____

_____

_____

_____

_____

_____

_____

_____

_____

_____

_____

LISTEN:

Let your mentee reveal their needs, hopes, and desires for the JumpStart experience. Listen for concerns, fears, or hesitations. The better you listen to what your mentee is saying, the deeper they will let you go!

SECOND LEVEL QUESTIONS:

JumpStart is not a sermon or a Bible study.
You will share, and you will study the Word.
However, JumpStart is a directed,
interactive, application oriented
encounter between you, your mentee,
The Word, and the Holy Spirit.

SECOND LEVEL QUESTIONS:

Listen carefully to your mentee as you spend time talking about the Scriptures. Listen to the answers they give to the questions. Then, in a discerning and gentle way, ask the second level questions!

SECOND LEVEL QUESTIONS:

If you are reading about salvation,
ask your mentee when they
accepted Jesus Christ.
If you are talking about spiritual gifts and the
call to serve, ask your mentee about their
gifts, and where they would like to serve.

SECOND LEVEL QUESTIONS:

Watch for body language.
Observe their countenance.
Discern when the Holy Spirit is speaking.
Do not rush, dig, or violate your mentee.
At the same time, do not hesitate to wait
on the Spirit and give Him time to work.

RELATIONAL INDUCTIVE BIBLE STUDY METHOD:

You do not need to take your mentee through the three page handout you received as part of mentor training. However, you should introduce your mentee to the four questions, and your role as mentor.

THE QUESTIONS:

What did the text mean back then?
What does it mean today?
What is it saying to me?
What must I do?

THE MENTORS ROLE:

The mentor stands alongside the mentee
to help them discern what God
is saying through His Word.
Then the mentor gently, prayerfully,
and patiently helps the mentee
discern how to put it into practice.

IT IS A JOURNEY:

JumpStart has sixteen sessions which can
easily take six months to complete.
Do not rush or force the experience.
Trust the material to lead you into sections
of the Word where the Spirit can speak!

IT IS A JOURNEY:

Allow God to set the pace.
Allow God to set the depth.
Stay on track with the sessions.
Stay in prayer.
Stay in the Word.
Stay in relationship with your mentee!

IT IS A JOURNEY:

If you establish strict expectations for your
mentee expect to be frustrated.
If you submit yourself, your mentee,
and the JumpStart process
to the Spirit of God
you will be amazed
by the places
He leads you!

Matthew 13:31-33 (NLT)

Here is another illustration Jesus used: "The Kingdom of Heaven is like a mustard seed planted in a field. It is the smallest of all seeds, but it becomes the largest of garden plants; it grows into a tree, and birds come and make nests in its branches."

Jesus also used this illustration: "The Kingdom of Heaven is like the yeast a woman used in making bread. Even though she put only a little yeast in three measures of flour, it permeated every part of the dough."

PART TWO:
Introduction to the Jethro/Moses Mentoring Model.

I am sixty-one years old and still learning to speak with people. You might say I have been in a forty-year period of recovery. My father was in the Military Police. I have been a Green Beret, Police Officer, car salesman, Special Events Director, and Lead Pastor. My earliest mentoring conversations took place with combat veteran Green Beret Master Sergeant J.C. Cooper. They were not really conversations. Most of the time J.C. talked and I listened. Then Dwayne Bruce was my Glendale Police Department Training Officer. Again, he taught and I listened. When I became a pastor, I assumed Christians wanted to hear the truth, have honest conversations, and grow into maturity with Jesus. It took many years for me to discover my foolish mistake. Over the years, I have participated in talks that went well. Other times they became a train wreck.

All good talks share some common ground with the pivotal conversation Jethro, the priest of Midian, had with his son in law Moses, the leader of God's people in the Exodus. We will carefully examine the steps Jethro and Moses took in their history altering time together. Moses was leading the children of Israel through the wilderness. He was doing everything himself, and burning out. The people were frustrated, and I suspect things were on the verge of getting ugly. In that pivotal moment Jethro, the father in law comes walking in from the desert for a visit.

This book is a companion volume to JumpStart. It is specifically written with the JumpStart mentor, or small group leader in mind. However, the principles and stories are timeless. They have application to business, church, sports, marriage, parenting, or simple friendships. I will confess some personal strengths and some weaknesses as we explore this amazing experience known as mentoring, or discipleship.

One good conversation literally has the power to change the trajectory of your life. I can think of multiple moments in my life where the chemistry was right, and transformation took place. One took place in the office of an Army recruiter. Another took place on a mountaintop in Puerto Rico. One conversation with Karen led to 38-years of marriage. The one in my pastor's office sent me to school. Another conversation, in my mentor's office, kept me in school. Two special conversation sent me from Fresno, CA to a seminary on the East coast. Conversations in a Poconos cottage guided my internship and set the bar for integrity in ministry. Talks with my D. Min. Mentor radically changed my view of the church, ministry, and Christ's Kingdom. One moment birthed JumpStart.

I pray this book gives you steps, and tools, to help you have the most God honoring and life changing conversations possible. If you are a mentor, pastor, teacher, or coach read from the perspective of Jethro. Examine the pattern he followed in his ministry to Moses. If you are a staff member, student, mentee, or new believer allow this book to give you the attitude and wisdom of Moses.

In some dimensions of our lives, we are Jethro. In others, we are Moses. There are principles in the passage we will explore which transcend position, and have the power to challenge each one of us. No matter who we are, and no matter what ministry God has called us to do. May God richly bless you, feed you, encourage you, and challenge you as you spend time with Jethro and Moses. Warning: This story has the potential to explode a pastors, churches, or denominations traditional view of leadership, duties, and church structure. I am praying it does. If this section stirs your soul connect it with Acts 6:1-7.

To do!

Take a moment and think about the personal issues going on in your life. Is there somebody you need to speak with? Is there somebody who needs to speak with you? Is there a situation in your family, workplace, sports team, or church? Write a note to yourself describing the situation. Revisit it when you finish JumpStart, and see if Jethro or Moses helped. I pray the Spirit of God meets you in His Word and speaks clearly!

THE ANNOUNCEMENT
Chapter Five

Early in my ministry at NorthPoint a senior Ministry Leader asked for a formal office appointment. We normally chatted in the hall so this request raised my attention level. A few days later the Chairman of the Board said to me in passing, "See you Tuesday." I enquired and learned I was meeting with the Chairman, Department Chair, and Ministry Leader. Turns out there was a long running feud between two Departments. I was young, and probably brash, so I simply invited the other Department Chair and Ministry Lead to the party. I probably would not do the same thing today. But I still hate being ambushed.

I love meeting with anyone about anything if you will simply tell me what you want to talk about and who is coming. On another occasion a pillar of the church walked into my office, laid a small tape recorder on the table, pressed record and said to me, "I have some questions." Today I would have told them any conversation requiring a tape recorder also required a couple of trusted Board Members. I was young, trusting, and optimistic so I answered his questions. Sadly, the taped conversation made the rounds of all the pillars of the church and fueled the fires that threatened to derail the ministry.

It is such a small courtesy to offer, and to expect. "Hey Bob, we have been thinking about spaceships invading earth. Can Bill and I buy you a cup of coffee Wednesday and pick your brain?" There is no stress, no drama, no angst, and no ambush.

Jethro told Moses who was coming to see him. This probably was not necessary in this setting. It may have just been a courtesy, or a formality. However, I have been in the awkward pastoral position of preparing for a meeting, and then seeing an unexpected entourage enter my office. I have learned over the years to let people know whom I am bringing to a meeting. Ambushes are effective for harming an enemy, but they rarely win over a friend. If I am going to meet with an adversary to have a potentially confrontational conversation I would like to know so that I may fairly and properly prepare for the encounter. Also, so all the right people are at the meeting to make the most of the time.

This is especially true in a mentoring conversation where trust and respect are the foundational building blocks for the relationship. In most cases, when a mentor meets with a mentee, they are in a long-term relationship. While sparks may occasionally fly the general tenor of their time together should be comfortable. Two comfortable armchairs, in a room free of pets, televisions, and small children is a good starting point for a meaningful conversation. Hot coffee, cold tea, or a bite of lunch can improve almost any conversations.

Then, before you go to the meeting do your homework. Jethro "heard about everything God had done for Moses and his people." He may or may not have known what he wanted to say to Moses, but he at least knew Moses's situation. It is embarrassing when somebody is caught trying to speak wisdom into a situation they know nothing about. It is like the American Congressman who went to Israel. He was offering his words of wisdom in the military command center. An Israeli general took him to the map on the wall and asked him to point out where he was. The map was not in English. When the Congressman admitted that he did not know, the general politely suggested he go home! The story may or may not be true but the point is rock solid. If you tell me why we are meeting, or I tell you, then we have time to prepare.

I have a board member with the Strengths Finder strength of "deliberation." For a while I thought this man just liked to string me along. Now the joke is that the board can discuss Monday, and we will get an email from brother Doug on Wednesday. Doug loves me, the board, the church, and Jesus. He is not against us, nor is he dragging his feet. He just likes to think things through before he speaks. I am an auditory processor. When things come out of my mouth my brain evaluates them. I process and adjust in the moment. Most don't work that way. If we give Doug notice prior to a meeting it gives him time to reflect, and be ready. Then we get his best input.

Have you ever been blindsided or ambushed in a meeting? What did it feel like?

_____

_____

_____

_____

_____

Has your experience in church meetings, leadership settings, or pastoral encounters always been positive?

_____

_____

_____

_____

I pray your church experience has always been positive, kind, honest, healing, loving, and redemptive. However, I have spoken with enough believers to know that is not always the case. Is there any root of bitterness from the past you need to let go of so God can fully use you in the present and future?

_____

_____

_____

_____

_____

_____

_____

_____

_____

_____

MEETING, GREETING, AND SEATING
Chapter Six

Exodus 18:7 (NLT)
So Moses went out to meet his father-in-law.
He bowed low and kissed him.
They asked about each other's welfare
and then went into Moses' tent.

Small talk and common courtesy can be an art form. They can also be a disaster. I was selling cars at Trans Ocean VW in Sierra Madre, CA around 1983. A thirty-something husband and wife walked confidently onto the lot and headed straight for a VW Camper. The man told me he and his wife had been looking at campers and liked the VW. This was awesome for several reasons. The VW Camper was expensive and would produce a great paycheck. Also, I owned one. Mine was older and nowhere near the price of the new one, but I was an experienced camper. I had traveled through Europe for six weeks during my teens in a VW Camper. I was very confident this sale was a slam dunk. Their car, clothes, and demeanor prequalified them as capable buyers.

I showed off the driver's area and the passenger's seat. We explored the back, made the bed, and raised the pop-up. We were standing behind the VW when I began my brilliant close. I raised the back door which revealed an awesome rectangular space. The space had the back of the upraised seat for a cushion. I explained to the couple what a perfect camping bassinet this area would make for their new baby. "With the back door locked of course," I added.

The woman turned without a smile and stormed off the lot. The husband gave me a sheepish grin, and in a low voice said, "She isn't pregnant." I felt bad about insulting the woman, and about losing a great commission. Nowadays I wait until I am in the delivery room to talk about anybody's new baby.

What is the point?
Moses went out to greet his father in law.
He bowed low and kissed him.
They asked about one another's welfare.
Then they went into the tent.

Their greeting, meeting, talking, and sharing was ice breaking. Even though Moses had spent forty years tending Jethro's sheep, was married to his daughter, and was the father of his grandsons he followed a polite course of etiquette.

My emotional happy place is no longer physically accessible to me. A prominent news caster purchased it when my grandparents moved to a retirement home. He does not know me and if I showed up asking to sit in his den things might not go well. It was different when my grandparents lived there. I lived in their house as a boy and slept on the old sofa in the den. It was the old kind of sofa that clicked when you pulled the back down. The back released and laid flat. You could then raise the front to remove the wool blankets that lived in the space below. Since the wool blankets were packed in mothballs the couch always had a very specific odor. The fireplace across from the coach burned for much of the winter. My grandfather loved oak the best so there was usually a great red bed of coals to light the room with their glow as I went to bed.

When I was a Glendale Police Officer my beat took me past my grandparents' house. There were no cell phones yet but my watch knew exactly what time lunch or dinner was. When grandpa saw my squad car pull up out front he would call for grandma to set another TV tray. When I sat on that old couch time stood still. I could speak with my grandparents about anything. I was loved in that house. It was the safest place in my world. I still confess to driving by occasionally when I am in Glendale. The front of the house looks pretty much the same. If I close my eyes I can smell the coach, hear the fire, and see my grandpa in his chair smoking a cigar while grandma finishes preparing a meal.

The setting of any conversation is of great importance. The time, place, environment, and people present may well determine the success or failure of the venture. Please do not try and speak with me if I am hungry, thirsty, tired, annoyed, or distracted. There are times when conversations, and teaching moments, must occur under terrible circumstances. People have yelled at me in warehouses, airplanes, boats, and police cars. However, if you have the time to pick the location make it comfortable, gentle, quiet, and conducive to the mentoring you want to conduct.

Other encounters may be one-time events with the power to determine destiny. In 1991, I was living in Fresno, California. The seminary I had been attending closed and the job I was working disappeared. I was seeking God's will but not making much progress. Judy was the secretary to the Senior Pastor of People's Church. She told me in a very authoritative way that I needed to see the Pastor. G. L. Johnson had thousands of members to watch over, but somehow he made a place for me in his schedule. I remember being afraid and impressed as I walked into the large office of the Senior Pastor of a large church.

I remember being immediately comfortable in his office, and in his presence. There was no intimidation, or posturing. There was just a very quiet confidence, and a deep sense that we were together to meet with Jesus, and to do something very important. G.L. asked me to tell my story. He listened intently as I shared about different schools, churches, and denominations. He did not interrupt, check his watch, play with his phone, or dig in his desk. He looked at me and listened to me as if we were the only two people on the planet. I talked about accepting Christ under a Pentecostal Chaplain, serving at JFK Memorial Chapel, attending L.I.F.E. Bible College, Azusa Pacific University, Fuller Seminary, an independent church, a charismatic seminary, and being licensed in a traditional Baptist Church. I was married to Karen at Forest Lawn Cemetery by a Four-Square preacher. When I completed my story G.L. smiled warmly and spoke words which literally gave me direction and changed the trajectory of the rest of my life. He said, "Everybody loves you but nobody wants you. There is a good old boy system, and you are not in it. You need to pick a denomination, attend their premier seminary, and when you graduate your gifts will make a place for you."

I am sitting in the mountains above Fresno, CA while I write this. I drove past People's Church on the way to where I am. It has been over twenty-five years since I heard those few sentences. I have tears in my eyes as I write because I know beyond question that the Holy Spirit opened his mouth to speak and my ears to hear. Thank you, Judy, for making me take the appointment. Thank you G.L. for listening and speaking God's Word into my heart. One man, one hour, one conversation, and one life changed. Or, is it possible JumpStart would not exist if I had not headed to Eastern Baptist Seminary and First Baptist Woodstown to serve under Dr. Howard Taylor. Or the twenty-one years I spent at NorthPoint. Maybe only Jesus knows what that one hour meant to His Kingdom!

How are you at meeting, greeting, and listening?
How well do you set the stage for conversations
so important that only eternity knows their value?

_____

_____

_____

_____

_____

_____

_____

_____

_____

_____

_____

_____

SHARE YOUR STORY
Chapter Seven

Exodus 18:8 (NLT)
Moses told his father-in-law everything the LORD had done
to Pharaoh and Egypt on behalf of Israel.
He also told about all the hardships
they had experienced along the way
and how the LORD had rescued his people from all their troubles.

I read about a woman who made up a story and went out visiting pastors. Sadly, I do not remember where I read this. However, she would go into the pastor's office begin her story and secretly start a stopwatch. She reported the average pastor listened for 90 seconds, then began talking. I was sitting on the wall of Thousand Pines Christian Camp and Conference Center many years ago. It was late at night and there were several of the college age staff sitting around. We were exploring their hopes and dreams. I love asking young people, "What school are you going to? What are you studying? What do you want to be when you grow up?" This happens in restaurants with the waitress or waiter, the car wash, fast food, airports, grocery stores, or anywhere. One of the camp staff said to me, "Pastor Paul, thanks for taking the time to speak with us." I responded they must talk to pastors all the time. Their response hurt my heart. "No, they are usually too busy and don't really want to talk to us." Ouch!

Moses told his father in law "everything the Lord had done." It was a long story. Jethro sat and listened to it all. He heard about the conflict, the escape, the rescue, and the hardships. Twenty minutes would be a short sharing of the Exodus. An hour would be legit. Throw in questions and this would have been a lengthy conversation. But Jethro listened. If Jethro had cut him off, changed the subject, or checked his sundial I doubt Moses would have continued to tell him "everything."

My friend Michael is a mentor, coach, pastor, and retired Army Sergeant Major. We met in 1978 and reconnected miraculously again in 1992. I can call Michael anytime and pour out my heart. He is a listener, and a lover of God. Michael will ask questions and suck the entire story out of me. My friend Dave is the same way. He will ask me how I am doing, and then he will listen until I am done. I never feel cut off or rushed. I feel listened to, affirmed, loved, and cared for. And when Dave or Michael speak I am ready to respect and hear whatever they want to tell me. They paid their listening dues and earned the right to speak freely into my life, for as long as they want, without me cutting them off or being done. They are men who answer Job's cry. **Job 31:35A (NLT) "If only someone would listen to me!"**

During my time at First Baptist Church in Woodstown, NJ, I had the privilege of working under Dr. Howard Taylor. He was my lab center supervisor during the final two years of my M. Div. at Eastern Seminary. [Now Palmer Seminary.] Howard had a cottage in the Pocono Mountains of East Pennsylvania. Some of my most spiritual conversations and moments of authentic transparency, took place while driving in a car, sitting beside a lake, and walking to the beaver dam down near the river. Howard and I were away from the office, beyond phones, and away from people. We could spend a couple days and nights reading, thinking, swimming, sailing, and talking. We could engage awhile, and then process privately. We were comfortable with one another's words, or silence. I do not know if Howard's mentoring was strategic, or just an organic expression of who he was. But I loved those times, and they deeply affected my soul.

Howard gave me one of the most profound learning moments of my life. I listened and learned because of his love for me. He listened so well and cared about me so much that Howard could have, and still can, tell me anything. We had a robust and difficult conversation about worship. It is safe to say we were intense with one another. A day or so later Howard called me into his office, sat me down, and asked me a life changing question. Keep in mind that he could have scolded me, fired me, or written me up. He did not. Instead he asked me a question.

On an intensity scale of 1-10, with ten being highest, where would you put yesterday's conversation? I thought a minute, and said, "A three or a four." Howard told me he was at an eight or nine. I laughed. Howard asked me to define my 1-10 conflict scale. Keep in mind I have been a soldier and a policeman. Considering my training and experience I told Howard one or two was a fun, nothing going on talk. Three is engaged in something of worth. Four is a passionate even boisterous engagement without anger. Five to six has a growing level of emotion. Seven sees the potential of physical engagement, anger, and raised voices. Eight probably involves pushing, wrestling, and defending. Nine is hitting, fighting, scrapping, and full physical engage. A progressive level of weapons appears. At ten somebody dies.

Howard was shocked. He was not a yeller, had never been in a fight, and the thought of hitting somebody with a club or shooting them was nowhere in his wheel house. It was an amazing moment of revelation. One I have never forgotten. When I am loud, engaged, and having a great time debating it is very possible normal people who have not spent time in a Green Beret hand to hand combat pit might be uncomfortable. This is one of those lessons I am still working on. The point is that people who listen to our stories, and ask questions, have the potential to work transformational learning into our lives.

How do you do at listening? Do you fully engage? Let people finish? Or are you a watch checking drawer cleaning texting machine?

_____

_____

_____

_____

_____

_____

_____

_____

_____

_____

_____

_____

_____

_____

_____

_____

_____

_____

_____

_____

_____

_____

_____

_____

_____

A WHOLE-HEARTED MENTOR
Chapter Eight

Exodus 18:9 (NLT)
Jethro was delighted when he heard about
all the good things the LORD had done for Israel
as he rescued them from the hand of the Egyptians.

The Apostle Paul challenges us to "Be happy with those who are happy, and weep with those who weep." Romans 12:15 (NLT) Sadly, many people including Christians do a much better job of weeping with those who weep than they do with being happy, or rejoicing, with those who rejoice.

Maybe it is jealousy, insecurity, smallness, meanness, upbringing, class envy, or something deeper. But for whatever reason there are people who cannot rejoice at the good fortune of others. I have watched people get a car, job, house, promotion, inheritance, ministry, or other blessing and have people react negatively. Sometimes people go down the "Why not me?" road. Why didn't I get a new car, house, job, etc.? Other times it is subtly spiritual. Did you need that car, house, job, etc.? Then there is the silent sulker. When joy is shared and a happy heart testifies, gloomy silence is deadly. The look on my face and the silence of my lips can throw a wet blanket on the glorious moment of another.

Maybe Jethro actually lived his priesthood. [Exodus 3:1] Perhaps he understood the importance of family relationships. His success in business as a sheep owner with employees may have broadened the scope of his own personhood. We do not know enough to say why, but Jethro was a spiritually magnanimous man who could "delight" in everything God had done. Jethro was a life giver, not a joy stealer.

In 2007 Karen and I had a stock go way up. Selling the stock would have created a huge tax burden. With the counsel of financial advisors, family, friends, and a church board we bought a larger house. It was a beautiful house. My plan was to sell stock each year, pay it off, and reap the tax benefit. When the economy went south the stock went to zip. In 2010 we were forced to give our dream home back to Cal Vet.

It is enlightening to look back on the journey of buying, building, and losing our home. Our friends were happy for us. They came to the house under construction and walked the land, prayed, and dreamed with us. We spoke of Life Groups and barbecues. Others reacted very differently. One young man of the church bitterly accused me of lying to the congregation. "How," I asked. "You told the congregation you were moving to the City of Highland," he answered. "I am!" said I. "No, you are moving into East Highlands

Ranch." I responded, "East Highland's Ranch is a Homeowners Association. I am moving to the city of Highland. And besides, the people of the church are helping me move. How can I lie to people about where I live when they are coming to my house and helping me move?" That is not a good way to keep a secret.

I was caught in the logic of the moment and did not realize we were talking about a heart issue. This young man was mad, jealous, and put out by the fact that I was buying a nicer house than his in a little better area. He already lived in Highland, but not East Highlands Ranch Home Owners Association. I have never dwelt on the fact, but to him it was a bone of contention. He eventually left the church, parked on the fact that I was a liar.

Others in my family, church body, and circle of friends celebrated as we moved in and wept with us when we moved out. It is sad to look back and realize the impact of joyful events on relationships. Coworkers can become bitter over salaries or promotions. Athletes can melt down over who plays a position. The jealousy between prima ballerina and understudy is legendary. Even in the church there can be distress over who gets the lead in an area of ministry.

It is essential as mentors that we check our insecurities, petty jealousies, and issues at the door. Our calling and privilege is to be the biggest champion our mentee has ever known. Our mentee will never open-up and share their hopes, dreams, and fears until they know it is completely safe to do so. Jethro's joyful security allowed Moses's honesty.

In the Hebrew language Jethro *hada* with Moses. He rejoiced, he was glad, and he joined with him in celebrating what God had done. When something good happens with your mentee you should rejoice, be glad, and join them in their joyful moment. When you lift them up you give them ever greater permission to open-up.

A little introspection and self-analysis. How do you do at rejoicing with those who rejoice? Are there things you might need to overcome in your own life to effectively mentor another?

_____

_____

_____

_____

_____

_____

_____

FOOD, GOD, AND WORSHIP
Chapter Nine

> Exodus 18:12 (NLT)
> Then Jethro, Moses' father-in-law,
> brought a burnt offering and sacrifices to God.
> Aaron and all the elders of Israel came out
> and joined him in a sacrificial meal in God's presence.

Who and how Jethro worshiped is beyond the scope of this project. I assume by chapter 18 Moses has an ever-growing understanding of Who he is serving. When Jethro brings his offerings, and sacrifices to God I accept he is offering to the God of Israel, and Moses his host. Anything else would have been insulting. When Aaron and the elders join the sacrificial meal it strongly suggests Yahweh is indeed the deity in whose presence and honor the meal is being eaten. With that said, allow me to draw freely and widely from the text.

Food can change the tempo and setting of a mentoring conversation. Coaches yell at players on the field and busy bosses often bark at subordinates in the office. These can be quick "bam-bam" kinds of interactions. It is possible for food to be a quick "bam-bam" in and out type of experience. But if used properly a meal can change everything.

My earliest memory of the table takes me back to my grandparents' home. Bruno drove for Weber's Bread in the 1950's and could bring home the "day old bread." My earliest childhood breakfast memories include the smell of coffee, toast, butter, and jam. Apricot-peach preserves on hot sour dough bread dripping with butter still remind me of the wood grained cupboards, red tiled linoleum, and four burner stove top being used to heat the kitchen. The pocket doors were closed to keep in the heat as we sat at the small breakfast table. Mornings are hurried, but they were still warm and intimate in that cozy setting.

Formal dinners at my grandparents were quite different. Granma cooked the roasted potatoes, vegetable, and biscuits. Grampa participated by watching the meat. When it was time to carve, it was all about me and grandpa on the service porch. The cutting board sat on the washing machine just through the door leading out of the kitchen. I was a co-conspirator in the magic moment when the marvelous end crust was cut or pulled off whatever glorious treasure came out of the oven. Ham at Easter, turkey at Christmas, and an occasional roast beef or rack of lamb. Those first bites on the back porch with my grandpa were magic.

When the adults came to table in the dining room I always took the seat to my grandfather's left. Tucked in the corner I was the only child listening to the adult conversation. Wine, dinner, dessert, and coffee with real cream and real sugar. Debates about sports, politics, and family business. I loved the amazing times of conversation, and family bonding. Those experiences established the model in my mind for what a meal can and should be. There could be amazing debate, even raised voices about the Rams, Lakers, stupid Republicans, or those damn Democrats. Grandpa was a Teamster and Uncle Harold was in management at the Gas Company. They could not be further apart politically. But the time I spent at that table taught me we were always family. Nothing said at that table would ever keep any of those people from rushing to my side no matter what my need. The table was a perfectly safe place.

The only thing missing from my grandparents table was God. When we grew up God was not part of the story. My namesake Uncle had been killed crossing San Fernando Road on his way to visit Bruno at the bakery. It was not until I was a believer home from the Army that I learned of my grandfather's pain and anger with God. "Who is God to take away my little boy?" he asked one night. The only answer I could give was to say "The one who gave His only son to pay for your and my sins on a cross."

Years later, when I was preparing for ministry, my grandfather got in my face and declared, "If you are going to be a preacher you will need to ask men if they know Jesus." I responded by looking my beloved grandfather right in the eyes and asking him, "Do you know Jesus?" He sat quietly for a few minutes, then looked back and quietly said "Yes."

I think God used my children to bring Him back to our extended family table. We would be in the home of extended family and my little kids would look around and say, "Aren't we going to pray before we eat?" One by one the dominos began to fall. Prayer became a part of almost every family meal.

Today I am the oldest male blood member of the Sandifer, Christensen, and Reinhard clans. I now have the privilege, duty, right, and responsibility of bringing God to the table. We talk about the Nativity at Christmas and the Resurrection at Easter. "What did you learn in Kids Connection today?" is always a fair question for Sunday lunch.

You must always measure the group you are with, the level of mentoring intimacy you have achieved, and the appropriateness of the surroundings. But when the time is right invite God to be front and center for your mentoring meal. Meals and conversions can be powerful in many ways in and of themselves. But when you, your mentee, or your group gather for God and food there will be a Holy openness and intimacy rarely matched by any other setting. When your mentee is ready, do not miss the opportunity to bring another man or woman, as appropriate, into your circle. The trust, peace, relationship, and table fellowship you share will be felt and experienced by the new addition. The experience may well open the door for a mentoring relationship of their own. If you are in a secular setting such as business, you can always bow your head for a silent moment. If the person you are with opens the door with a question, walk in. Otherwise, just eat.

(Warning: If you are mentoring a member of the opposite sex out of necessity beware the hidden pitfall inherent in the intimacy of eating. When I was a youth pastor at Sunland Baptist Church I met my female intern in the front booth of Jack in the Box. An older member once asked me if that was a good idea. I answered, "Yes, my office is tucked up in a back corner of the second floor of the sanctuary. It is empty most of the time. My wife and Senior Pastor know exactly what time and day to look for me in the front window of the Foothill Blvd Jack in the Box. It was a short walk away so no cars were involved. It was the perfect place to meet my young, attractive college intern.)

A sacrificial meal shared by a group can become more than a conversation. I am going to dare and call it worship. Think of Jesus breaking bread with the masses. Or Jesus with the twelve at the last supper. Something tremendously powerful happened. This can happen in your family circle with Christmas, Easter, or Thanksgiving. Songs or scripture can deepen, enrich, and expand the meaning of normal gatherings. Use wisdom in secular settings, but when appropriate, God may still be invited to the table with care.

Reflection:

What memories does the family table have for you? For some of you this will be easy. Others of you have painful memories of failed family relationships. Allow my story to open your heart to a new model. Be open to healing and learning a new tradition.

_____

_____

_____

How might you bring God into your table time?

_____

_____

_____

How can God become more prominent at the family festivals you oversee?

_____

_____

One more Thought:

Over the years God has brought people, especially young couples, into Karen's and my life. We have adopted kids who spend birthdays, holidays, and any days in our home. They have "refrigerator rights." The older I get the more I understand the blessing my birth family was to me. Be aware that your mentee, or others God brings you, might need you to model a whole new way of doing family. Your love and acceptance has amazing power.

ASK THE QUESTION
Chapter Ten

> **Exodus 18:14 (NLT)**
> When Moses' father-in-law saw
> all that Moses was doing for the people,
> he asked, "What are you really accomplishing here?
> Why are you trying to do all this alone
> while everyone stands around you from morning till evening?"

It is critical to see we are in chapter six and the issue is about to come up. Jethro and Moses greeted, shared, listened, ate, worshiped, and connected. Now, multiple layers into the process, Jethro is going to pop the question. I realize this pattern is not always possible. This does not work in combat training, day to day office work, the football practice field, or even parenting your children. But if Jethro's time with Moses was the tipping point in the younger man's ministry then the model has veracity for all of us in some way.

Years ago, my wife worked in the church office. People would walk in and bark nonsense to her. Way too many fonts in the bulletin. The music was too loud. The pastor was too long. Whatever! Karen would vent to me later, "It is all in the approach!" She did not usually mind what the people had to say, the issue was how they said it.

Jethro spent time with Moses. He shadowed him. There was firsthand knowledge of the problem. And let me say again, there was greeting, meeting, eating, sharing, listening, worship, and deep connection. In that context of respect Jethro throws out the probe, "What are you REALLY accomplishing here and WHY are you TRYING to do ALL this ALONE?" If we turned the text and allow it to speak directly it might say, YOUR TRYING TO DO THIS ALL BY YOURSELF AND NOT ACCOMPLISHING ANYTHING!

This question goes to the very center of a man's life, calling, and sense of accomplishment. I suggest there is an introspective depth to this question containing the power to shatter a lessor man's ego. Imagine your boss, spouse, coach, or colleague looking you square in the eye's when you are doing the most important thing you do and asking, "What are doing? What are you accomplishing? Why are you doing the most important thing you think you do the way you are doing it? Why, if you're the leader, are all these other people standing around?" The not so subtle inference is that you are messing up! OUCH!

I do not know about you, but those questions would certainly have the potential of blowing me up! Yet, Jethro was willing to ask it.

How do you do when somebody gets in your space, and makes a pointed observation?

_____

_____

_____

_____

_____

Now, turn it around. How do you handle people getting all "Up in your business?"

_____

_____

_____

_____

_____

Does the approach make any difference? What do you want from people who are speaking into your life? How can you do better at speaking into the life of others?

_____

_____

_____

_____

_____

Thought:

Each of us is different. Some people handle brutal correction like water off a duck's back. Others wither and shut-down after a simple word. You will learn about your mentee as you go along. It is always better to speak gently, and explore the boundaries of the relationship slowly. You are on a journey together. Avoid burning the long-term relationship by prematurely delivering a short-term word. Pray for wisdom always, and trust God to guide you. Remember the section on body language. It can be a good indicator of your mentees receptiveness. Keys in the hand, texting, and looking at the window indicate they are probably done with the conversation. Catch the clues and save your thoughts for another time.

ANSWER THE QUESTION
Chapter Eleven

> Exodus 18:15-16 (NLT)
> Moses replied,
> "Because the people come to me to get a ruling from God.
> When a dispute arises, they come to me,
> and I am the one who settles the case
> between the quarreling parties.
> I inform the people of God's decrees
> and give them his instructions."

In 1980 I was hired by the Glendale Police Department and sent to the Los Angeles County Sheriff's Academy Class 200. Physical fitness was an essential element of our training. Remembering to bring a towel for the showers was key to the program. The Training Officers made it very clear we were never ever, under any circumstances, to touch the racks of clean white folded fresh smelling laundered towels. After a long hot sweaty run through the rolling hills of East Los Angeles, in all our tactical gear, we were released to shower and dress for more classroom instruction. As I stripped off my stinky sweaty PT gear I realized I had forgotten to bring a towel. Since I am a creative problem solver I decided to take a used towel from the laundry basket. OK, I agree it is nasty and you can moan and judge if you want. But I was stinky sweaty nasty and in need of a shower. I had no towel. I dared not take a clean one from the Training Officers shelf. I did what I had to do. I showered, dried with a dirty towel, dressed, and returned to the classroom. I took my seat in the rows of cadets and waited for class to begin.

The Deputy walked out and began the class with a question. "Which of you stupid stinky
_____ _____ forgot your towel?" I sat in my seat with a terrible quandary playing out inside my head. Avoiding attention, stress, difficulty, and situations with Training Officers was key to survival. Against my better judgement, my hand went up. The Deputy told me to stand up. There I was standing amongst a room full of sitting cadets. This was my worst scenario come to life. All my training experience in the U.S. Army screamed at me for being in this high-profile moment.

The Deputy yelled at me for being a nasty human being who dried off with another stinky person's towel. The class laughed as the Deputy berated me. Then he looked at the class and asked, "Did anybody else forget your towel?" He waited to see if anyone responded. Nobody did. Then he spoke these fateful words. "Go get your towels!" He told me to remain standing while the rest of the class ran off to obey his command. As cadets returned the Training Cadre roamed the room checking for a towel. Those with towels were ordered to sit. Those returning without towels were ordered to stand. When everyone was in their place there were about seven cadets standing with me. The Deputy barked at me, "You're a dirty nasty _____ _____! But you're an honest _____ _____!" "SIT DOWN!" My ordeal was over. It had been short, ugly, and embarrassing. But it done. They were finished with me. The Deputies in the room turned withering stares and brutal words to the "LIARS" amongst us. The seven standing cadets endured extra PT, mental harassment, verbal abuse, and several of them ended up dropping out. I suffered no permanent damage.

When Jethro asked Moses what he was doing and what he was accomplishing it was probably an awkward moment for God's chosen leader. That question from his father-in-law could have made him mad, insecure, or embarrassed. It would have been easy for Moses to launch into a speech about who he was and how God had used him in a might way thus far. It would have been easy for him to pop off with something like, "You lead sheep. I lead men! Who are you to question me?" I have heard leaders use "I am God's man" to cover bad decisions and poor behavior. Your title or position is never justification for wrong behavior.

We do not know Moses's though process, or emotions, but we do see his answer. Moses gives an honest, accurate, reasonable, and straight forward account of his current leadership. He may share the blame with the people who are coming to him for answers. But for the most part he opens himself up for the word of correction which is about to come. Moses has the emotional, intellectual, and spiritual strength to handle rigorous self-assessment.

How do you handle the hard question? When your wife, parents, kids, boss, coach, or mentor asks you to give an account of what you are doing and why you are doing it, how do you respond? Are you like the teenager who responds to his parent's questions with answers like, "Out, later, friends, around, and I don't know?" Or do you own your actions and give a clear answer?

_____

_____

_____

_____

_____

_____

_____

If you have a hard time with vulnerability
try praying the prayer of David in Psalm 139:23-24 (NLT).

Search me, O God, and know my heart;
test me and know my anxious thoughts.
Point out anything in me that offends you,
and lead me along the path of everlasting life.

CAN YOU DRAW WHAT BEING VULNERABLE LOOKS LIKE?

A WORD OF CORRECTION
Chapter Twelve

> Exodus 18:17 (NLT)
> "This is not good!" Moses' father-in-law exclaimed.

In the fall of 1974 approximately one hundred and fifty men went out to Camp Mackall, NC for Phase One of Special Forces training. One month later twenty-eight appeared in the graduation photo. Some of the men quit while others returned to Ft. Bragg in an ambulance. Things got broken during training. In that violent world of running, hitting, climbing, and parachuting the thought of being hurt by words is absurd.

During my stay in the U.S. Army I was yelled at, cursed at, screamed at, and berated. I was also pumped up and encouraged. Things often happened in the moment. No preparation beforehand and no reflection after the fact. If the man above me wasn't climbing fast enough I would yell. If the man behind was lagging, we would yell. If things went well, we would yell. We were loud, colorful, direct, and completely unfiltered. One moment you might be a sweet _____ _____. The next you might be a stupid _____ _____.

The Sheriff's academy was not as intense, but it was still pointed and colorful. Bad language, dirty stories, and personal slams were par for the course. Bodies were not broken as often, but the hand to hand contact was physical and combative. We were being trained to restrain and handcuff citizens who did not wish to go with us. When you encountered a combative citizen, physical contact was necessary.

A combination of family, military, and police training gave me a singular communication style. I was prone to talk before listening. I was trained to use my command voice and maintain control of the situation. I could access, and react. Even today at sixty plus years of age I still have a hidden switch. In an emergency, I lose all insecurity, self-deprecation, and sensitivity. I can instantly move into order giving mode. Call 911. Stick your finger in that hole. Do this, do that.

But do this and do that do not work in the church. It might be effective for a moment in a short-term high stress situation. But it will not bear fruit in long term relationships.

For years, I bottled up my frustration, anger, and judgment. At home and at church it happened like this. I was a very peaceful guy. But I feared conflict and unpleasant situations. I knew my ability to take a conversation straight up the conflict ladder. The longer I was in the church, and the more I desired to be a "Man of God" the more I kept a tight lid on my emotions, and opinions. And that caused a problem. My feelings, observations, and leadership gifts could not be silent. They simmered until something opened the can. Then out came my angst and opinions in totally unproductive ways. People's feelings were hurt. Ministries were hampered. I was pushed deeper in the cycle of observation, opinion, suppression, simmer, explode, regret, and new attempts to suppress.

About six years into my Doctor of Ministry I saw my pattern. I was devastated, frustrated, and relieved all at the same time. Then I discovered God had a very simple solution.

Ephesians 4:15-16 (NLT)
Instead, we will speak the truth in love,
growing in every way more and more like Christ,
who is the head of his body, the church.
He makes the whole body fit together perfectly.
As each part does its own special work, it helps the other parts grow,
so that the whole body is healthy and growing and full of love.

Speak the truth. To your spouse, kids, grandkids, board, leaders, and mentee. Do not simmer, brood, store up, or let things fester. Do not allow things to pressurize until they explode unproductively and cause terrible harm. Part of my special work as a husband, father, pastor, church leader, and mentor is to coach, counsel, train, and communicate with those in my life. It is my job, it is right, and I am missing God's best if I fail to do it.

Speak the truth, in love. We are to speak the truth in agape. Speak truth in the love that God gives, in the love God has for us. Speak the truth in a way that heals and helps people. Speak truth in such a way that the Body of Christ comes together perfectly, healthy, and growing. Speak without wounding, ripping, and harming. Even difficult things can be said productively if the others persons' best interest guides your thinking. And, if what you say is said gently, kindly, and in a loving fashion. Don't be depressed if this sounds out of reach. Mentors are on a journey just as much as the mentee. I still aspire to get these things right. Sometimes I do, and sometimes I don't.

When Dr. Wilson taught the existence of the reptilian brain stem it opened my eyes to me. This is the part of our being which causes our hand to catch a flying ball before we cognitively process the fact that it is about to smash our face. It is the response that puts our hand across our child's lap even as our foot is streaking for the brake. These lifesaving measures are awesome when functioning properly.

When they allow our ticked off emotions to use our mouth without consulting the frontal lobes of the brain it is terrible. Can you remember being an angry child and somebody telling you to count to ten. Turns out they were physiologically correct. Ten seconds allows the unfiltered electrical impulses of our reptilian brain stem to fade and our cognitive though process to engage and control our mouth before it does harm.

For the past several years I have been telling myself, "Speak sooner, speak kinder." Do not get sucked into an angry reptilian response. In the words of my grandfather, "Think before you speak." What an amazing concept. Slow it down, think, check your heart, filter your attitude. Do not bottle your thoughts and feelings up like a shaken can of Coke. When you are right, and the time is right, speak the truth in love.

Jethro greeted Moses, they had small talk, they ate, and they worshipped. Jethro spent time with Moses. He watched what was going on. He asked the pointed question. Then he listened to the answer. Then, and only then, did Jethro speak the words destined to transform the leadership style of Moses. "This is not good."

As I have said many times before in this book. This model is the ideal. You cannot follow every step every time. No army would march, no football offense would roll, and no office emergency would be immediately resolved. But for the mentor-mentee, pastor-congregation, husband-wife, and parent-child relationships the truth spoken in love after sensitive and careful preparation will bear tremendous fruit and prevent much relational pain and damage.

So:

How do you do when it is time to speak the pointed word?

_____

Do you relish the moment?

_____

Do you resist the moment?

_____

Do you store up your angst and explode?

_____

Does it come easy and natural for you?

_____

How can you do better at speaking the truth in love?

_____

_____

_____

A TIME TO TEACH
Chapter Thirteen

Exodus 18:18-22 (NLT)
"You're going to wear yourself out—and the people, too.
This job is too heavy a burden
for you to handle all by yourself.
Now listen to me,
and let me give you a word of advice,
and may God be with you.
You should continue to be
the people's representative before God,
bringing their disputes to him.
Teach them God's decrees,
and give them his instructions.
Show them how to conduct their lives.
But select from all the people some capable,
honest men who fear God and hate bribes.
Appoint them as leaders over groups
of one thousand, one hundred, fifty, and ten.
They should always be available to solve
the people's common disputes,
but have them bring the major cases to you.
Let the leaders decide the smaller matters themselves.
They will help you carry the load,
making the task easier for you.

This may be my favorite section of the story. The questions, defense, and confrontation are over. Now it is time to teach. I love to teach. People have told me part of my spiritual gifting is prophetic and discernment. A pastor I love told me some years ago I make people mad because I see things nobody else is seeing and speak them before people are ready to hear them. Somedays it is necessary to speak prophetically and directly to a situation. There are times when it is your duty to do so. Let me unpack this a bit and give you a rough example.

One night I drove my police car code three to a multiple shots fired men down call. The dispatcher noted there was a man with a shotgun seen running in the neighborhood. My partner and I rolled up. He ran across the street to tend the man kneeling on the ground who was bleeding and throwing up blood. I walked carefully unto the lawn of a house to check the man lying face down. I grabbed his arm to roll him over. It almost came off in my hand. I discerned the man was dead.

A few minutes later the front door opened and a man came running from the house reloading his 357 magnum. I drew my gun, took aim, and ordered him to freeze. "Lower your gun slowly to the ground!" It was a very clear prophetic teaching moment. He obeyed. It was a very good decision. We were not having a conversation. If his gun had moved any direction except for down, I would have shot him.

Gladly, this is the opposite of the teaching moment you will have with your mentee. You have eaten, prayed, loved, served, listened, watched, asked questions, and now it is time to teach. Enjoy this moment. When your mentee is ready open your heart and share your wisdom, advice, and encouragement. Tell your mentee what you see, and what you believe God is showing you.

Be wise, discerning, and gentle. Watch the body language of your mentee very carefully. Is there forehead relaxed or tight with wrinkles? Are their eyes relaxed, open, and focused on you? Or do they keep darting nervously toward the door or window? Are your mentees shoulders relaxed, or are they high and tight? What about their hands and arms? Are they folded in attention on the table? Are they relaxed and flopping? Or are their hands and arms folded, or stuck into their pockets? Are they busy combing their hair, looking in their purse, or organizing their wallet? Are they leaning forward attentively or slumped back, or down, in their chair? Are they standing up, pacing, or fidgeting in their chair? If you are in a car and they are playing with the radio, leaning against the door, arms folded, legs crossed, and looking out the side window, they may be done listening.

Use mentoring as a time to teach when appropriate, but always read the signs. If the man has a gun go 110% directive because you only have one shot, no pun intended. But if you are in a long-term JumpStart mentoring relationship you can teach slowly, progressively, and patiently. As the old saying goes, "You do not need to dump the whole load of hay on the one cow in one trip!" Too much, too soon, to rough, and you can burn the bridge forever. Resist the temptation to keep pressing if you encounter resistance.

Make your teaching moments so positive and affirming for your mentee that they joyfully covet your advice and input. My son always reminds me when I preach that it is better for people to feel shorted and want to come back next week than to bury them with so much information they need a month off. The same is true of your mentee. If you beat them with a stick every time you meet they will soon find excuses to be somewhere else. We humans are funny that way!

Think about people you have known. How did your family, teachers, or mentors speak into your life? What can you learn from their example?

_____

_____

_____

_____

_____

Think about who you are. Your personality, training, and general disposition. How do you teach others? Are you sensitive to what they are hearing, or just focused on what you are saying?

_____

_____

_____

_____

_____

Are their people, or areas, in your life that you should teach in a better way? How can you do this?

_____

_____

_____

_____

_____

IF GOD COMMANDS
Chapter Fourteen

> Exodus 18:23 (NLT)
> "If you follow this advice,
> and if God commands you to do so,
> then you will be able to endure the pressures,
> and all these people will go home in peace."

This may come as a surprise, but "YOU ARE NOT GOD, AND EITHER AM I." There are cults who become very toxic in this area of mentoring. I once asked a man to leave our church because he kept wanting to be the "Spiritual Covering" for women whose husbands were not Christian. I know of churches who decide who should date and marry whom. There are churches who tell people what news to watch, or not watch. We are not those people. We are servants and mentors, not spiritual oppressors. We suggest, not demand.

The first word in the passage, "IF" is tremendously important. In a church or ministry context the decision to accept and act upon advice is always in the hands of the mentee. Jethro told Moses things would go well "IF" he did what Jethro suggested. The word "IF" makes it clear that the choice to hear and act belonged to Moses. All Jethro could do was present, Moses had to receive. Jethro had no positional or spiritual authority over Moses other than trust, respect, and credibility built up over forty years of their family relationship.

Our role as mentors is to love people, serve people, explore the Bible with people, share our journey, our sins, and what we have learned on the way. We should speak when the door is opened, exhort correct teach when we are invited to do so, and intervene rarely and only with great cause. As I said in Part One, the mentee should set the level of the interaction. You are not their parent, boss, spouse, or spiritual covering. You are most likely not their pastor. If you are it adds other dimensions of ethical responsibility to the relationship. We serve, never seeking to own, control, or over direct.

At the end of the day every man or women is accountable to God. Now, I will admit my prophetic teaching gift, and my Strength Finder WOO incline me toward strong persuasion. Throw in a little cop and Green Beret and you can end up with a very opinionated salesman. Add in pastor shepherd and you can end up with a person having a tremendously high sense of knowing what is right, and what needs to done, and probably what you should do.

Having confessed all that let me shout again, "I AM NOT GOD, AND NEITHER ARE YOU." The people I mentor are ultimately accountable to God for their decisions, beliefs, and actions. I will argue intensely to the best of my ability for what I believe to be right but I will never violate the space, free will, or human dignity of my mentee.

The only exception is if I believe there is an imminent risk of harm or violence to themselves or another. In that case I compel you to go immediately to your pastor or trusted church leader and share your concerns. If you are the pastor I pray God gives you the wisdom and courage to do whatever is right, even if it harms the relationship or costs you a church member. It is always better to suffer for doing the right thing.

If you apply JumpStart mentoring principles in a context other than personal mentoring or ministry there is an important distinction. What I am about to say also applies in the church at the leadership level. If my mentee is not in my chain of leadership command, then everything in the previous chapters is correct.

If my mentee works for me, reports to me, leads ministry I am ultimately responsible for, or represents the organization I have a sworn duty to protect another principle comes into play. I still recommend the process we have been following as a healthy one for developing subordinates. However, if I am in charge there must be another level. It's called consequences. It comes from a cosmic principle called, "Cause and effect."

I work for God, and I report to God, and so there are times God calls me to take responsibility for my job, and His ministry, in a way that will have direct consequences for someone else. Let me give you an example.

If you are my mentee [but not in my chain of command] and we are working on your bad habit of drinking too much, sleeping in, being late to work, not performing, and negatively impacting your ministry, job, and family I will love you, teach you, pray for you, and eventually speak some firm words of correction to you, even if they risk our mentoring relationship. If you work for me I will invite you to attend a Celebrate Recovery meeting, get sober, get to work on time, become effective or face being fired. I will not violate your sovereignty. You are free to choose alcohol, tardiness, incompetence, and unemployment. After working through all the right redemptive processes to help you, my responsibility before the Lord will be to fire you. Now, I will still love you, and be available to you. But I will not feel morally responsible to pay your bills and separate you from the logical consequences of your choices. Being accountable to God is a two-edged sword.

Remember, when you teach, coach, counsel, correct or get directive with your mentee he/she is always living under the freedom and authority of their "IF." You are their mentor and friend, but only God is God. At the end of the day your mentee belongs to Him, not you. Keep that in mind and you will avoid becoming a crazy cult which embarrasses us all.

How do you do in the "If?" Another way of saying this is, "Do you have good boundaries in relationships?" Do you balance your responsibilities with another's personhood?

_____

_____

_____

_____

_____

Let's explore guilt and responsibility issues for just a moment. If you say or do something that puts somebody else in the position of choosing and living with the consequences is that a problem for you? How can you deal with this better?

_____

_____

_____

_____

_____

How will you handle sharing teaching with your mentee then allowing them to choose what to use? What if they don't?

_____

_____

_____

_____

_____

ABLE TO LISTEN
Chapter Fifteen

Exodus 18:24 (NLT)
Moses listened to his father-in-law's advice
and followed his suggestions.

Proverbs 16:18 (KJV)
Pride goeth before destruction, and an haughty spirit before a fall.

Proverbs 3:7-8 (NASB)
Do not be wise in your own eyes; Fear the LORD and turn away from evil.
It will be healing to your body and refreshment to your bones.

1 Peter 5:6 (NLT)
So humble yourselves under the mighty power of God,
and at the right time he will lift you up in honor.

Numbers 12:3 (NASB)
Now the man Moses was very humble,
more than any man who was on the face of the earth.

Please see we are deep into our mentoring model. This should be a great encouragement for you TYPE-A super motivated impatient over achievers who want your mentee to have gotten it yesterday. [Do not be insulted because I am one of you. I resonate with the poster of the two vultures sitting on the cactus. The caption reads, "PATIENCE MY _ _ _, LET'S GO KILL SOMETHING."]

See clearly that Jethro did not walk in out of the desert, drop his suitcase, and tell Moses how stupid he was and what a bad job he was doing. Jethro used the JumpStart Mentoring Model Conversation, which you now know we got from him, to connect with Moses and speak into his life. When you and I have done our absolute best, we must remember the results rest with God, and our mentee. It goes back to that thorny old issue of free will. I am not entering the age-old Calvinist debate so don't get derailed; I'm just saying people make decisions. Sometimes they choose well, other times they don't. How God factors into that for the fulfillment of His cosmic plan for the universe is way above my paygrade.

But do not miss the next verse I'm "fixen" to drop on "ya'll!" That's for my family and friends in Texas! Here it is now, get ready for it! The most important mentee verse in this whole dang book. If you get this truth, you will go far. If not then your capacity for illumination, self-discovery, and progress is extremely limited.

Numbers 12:3 (NASB)
(Now the man Moses was very humble, more than any man who was on the face of the earth.)

We have looked at the fact that a disciple is a learner. They are a student. Their goal is to sit at the feet of their master, learn from them, and become like them. There are people running around whose personal cup is so full of themselves there is no room for anybody to add anything to it. I know pastors like this. If you see them in a grocery store they talk about themselves and "their church" for twenty minutes without breathing. [Note: It's not their church. It's God's.] They have no interest at all in who you are, what you think, or what you might need from the meeting. All they care about is their own life and ministry. If you ask how they are doing, they respond with a sermon on the second coming of Christ. I confess avoiding them if I see them first.

Humble people are teachable. They are learners, listeners, and ready to hear the voice of God no matter where it comes from. I have been in the classroom with my now 87-year-old mentor. I have seen him teaching material from the core of his being and a student ask a question, or challenge him, and him smile and say "Alright, good point, what do you mean by that." Then he thinks about it, processes it, and if need be makes an adjustment. That is humility.

Years ago, Dr. Bill Bright, the founder of Campus Crusade for Christ, attended NorthPoint then Calvary Baptist, when he was visiting San Bernardino. I was brand new in my first Lead Pastor position when somebody told me excitedly that Dr. Bright is here this morning. I panicked at the thought of preaching to a man whose ministry touched the entire world. After a few visits I finally got up the courage to ask him, "What should I do when you're here? Would you like to preach, and I will just sit and listen? What do I do?" He smiled and took my hand.

"I just come here to worship Jesus with God's people. Since I have a large group that travels with me we will probably slip in a little late, sit in the back, and leave after the message so we do not disturb the service or create distraction. But if you ever need me to pray with you about anything Vonette and I are at your service." I remember going through a time of struggle. True to his word, Dr. Bright and Vonette stood with Karen and I in the church library. We held hands and this dear sweet man of God lifted us up to the throne of grace.

Reflect on his words. "I'll come a moment late, leave a moment early, so as not to cause a fuss. I just want to worship God with his people. But if you want to pray I'm here for you." That is the humble heart God takes and makes into a global leader. The amazing thing is he would sit in church, and take notes. That is one of the craziest things I have ever seen.

Dear sweet precious mentee. Your level of openness, of humility, of teach ability, and your vulnerability will directly determine how much you benefit from the mentor God has given you. Declaring you to be the gatekeeper, the one who sets the depth of the conversation is right and offers you a great protection. It also gives you a tremendous responsibility. You will get as much out of JumpStart as you put of yourself into it. I pray you throw wide your soul and walk boldly through the door God has put before you.

What do humility and teach ability look like to our artists?

THE RESULT
Chapter Sixteen

> Exodus 18:25-27 (NLT)
> He chose capable men from all over Israel
> and appointed them as leaders over the people.
> He put them in charge of groups of
> one thousand, one hundred, fifty, and ten.
> These men were always available
> to solve the people's common disputes.
> They brought the major cases to Moses,
> but they took care of the smaller matters themselves.
> Soon after this, Moses said good-bye to his father-in-law,
> who returned to his own land.

The optimistic outcome of a Jethro/Moses conversation is a peaceful relationship between the participants and a glorious transformation in the situation which created the need for the conversation. This story has the perfect outcome.

It appears Moses and Jethro are still friends. Moses experiences a breakthrough in ministry that allows him to remain the leader. Israel continues her journey with a new and improved leadership structure.

Sadly, not every conversation will end this way. I do not want to be negative but I want to encourage you mentors with the fact that some people love me and some people hate me. More love me than hate me at this stage of my life and ministry but there are several folks floating around who will probably not be coming to my funeral. They may come to the party afterwards, but not the funeral.

Seriously, even if you do your best the choice to listen and change is always in the hands of the mentee. You cannot save a lost soul, because only God has that power. In the same way, you cannot conform somebody to the image of Christ. Only the Word and Spirit of God can accomplish that miracle.

You can love, serve, share, pray, preach, listen, and passionately engage if needed. Only when someone surrenders to God will He produce fruit in their life. Put everything you have learned into practice, and then trust God. If things go well and your mentee soars, praise God and give Him the glory. If your mentee bails, fails, and falls flat trust God, and do not take the blame if you did your best.

Remember:
If you are not allowed to take the glory when things go well
then you are not allowed to take the blame if things go badly.

Jesus Christ had His Peter, James, and John.
He had His doubting Thomas.
He had his Judas.
Why should your ministry be any different?

The secret is for you to learn from your experiences,
and do it better next time!
Most of us do not do anything perfectly
the first time we try, or the second, or the third.

Besides, quitting on the call of Christ too go
into all the world and make disciples,
baptizing them in the name of the Father,
the Son, and the Holy Ghost,
and teaching them to obey all He taught,
is not really an option,
IS IT?

A MODEL MENTOR
CONVERSATION TRAINING
Chapter Seventeen

Mentoring did not begin in the N.T. Jesus was the ultimate disciple maker, but the God of Israel has a long history of raising up spiritual leaders. The O.T. gives us an awesome glimpse into one conversation in what was a long term mentoring relationship.
Moses was the "giver of the Law" and the "leader of the Exodus from Egypt."
In Exodus 18, we see Jethro, the priest of Midian and the father in law of Moses having a history changing conversation.

Exodus 18:7 (NLT)
So Moses went out
to meet his father-in-law.
He bowed low and kissed him.
They asked about each other's welfare
and then went into Moses' tent.

Exodus 18:8 (NLT)

Moses told his father-in-law everything
the LORD had done to Pharaoh
and Egypt on behalf of Israel.
He also told about all the hardships
they had experienced along the way
and how the LORD had rescued his
people from all their troubles.

Exodus 18:9 (NLT)
Jethro was delighted
when he heard about all the
good things the LORD had done
for Israel as he rescued them
from the hand of the Egyptians.

Exodus 18:12 (NLT)

Then Jethro, Moses' father-in-law, brought a burnt offering and sacrifices to God. Aaron and all the elders of Israel came out and joined him in a sacrificial meal in God's presence.

When Moses' father-in-law saw all that Moses was doing for the people, he asked,
"What are you really accomplishing here? Why are you trying to do all this alone while everyone stands around you from morning till evening?"

Exodus 18:15-16 (NLT)

Moses replied, "Because the people come to me to get a ruling from God. When a dispute arises, they come to me, and I am the one who settles the case between the quarreling parties. I inform the people of God's decrees and give them his instructions."

Exodus 18:17 (NLT)
"This is not good!"
Moses' father-in-law exclaimed.

What if Jethro had begun with
"This is not good"?

Exodus 18:18-23 (NLT)

"You're going to wear yourself out—and the people, too. This job is too heavy a burden for you to handle all by yourself. Now listen to me, and let me give you a word of advice, and may God be with you.

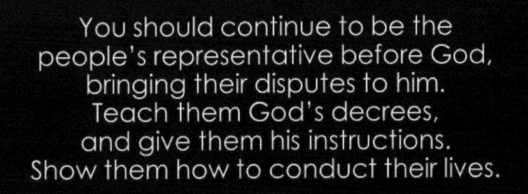

You should continue to be the
people's representative before God,
bringing their disputes to him.
Teach them God's decrees,
and give them his instructions.
Show them how to conduct their lives.

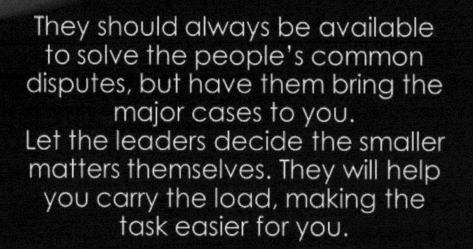

They should always be available to solve the people's common disputes, but have them bring the major cases to you.
Let the leaders decide the smaller matters themselves. They will help you carry the load, making the task easier for you.

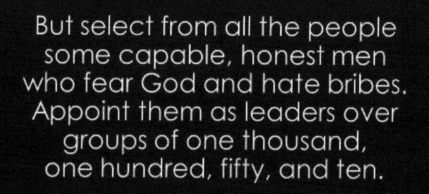

But select from all the people
some capable, honest men
who fear God and hate bribes.
Appoint them as leaders over
groups of one thousand,
one hundred, fifty, and ten.

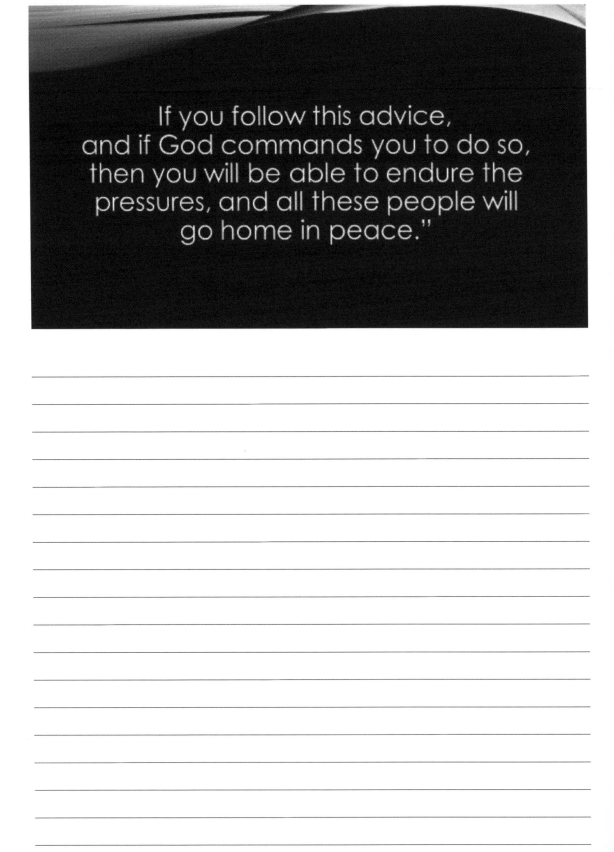

If you follow this advice,
and if God commands you to do so,
then you will be able to endure the
pressures, and all these people will
go home in peace."

Exodus 18:24 (NLT)
Moses listened
to his father-in-law's advice
and followed his suggestions.

MENTORS ATTITUDE

A.
How would you describe Jethro's spirit
during this encounter?
Why was this important?

_____

_____

_____

_____

_____

_____

_____

_____

_____

_____

_____

_____

_____

_____

_____

_____

_____

_____

THE MENTEE'S ATTITUDE

B.
What do you see
in the attitude of Moses during this
meeting? Why was this important?

_____
_____
_____
_____
_____
_____
_____
_____
_____
_____
_____
_____
_____
_____
_____
_____
_____

C.
Are you ready to invite someone
to speak honestly into your life?

_____

_____

_____

_____

_____

_____

_____

_____

_____

_____

_____

_____

_____

_____

_____

_____

_____

MINISTRY APPLICATION

D.
Are you ready to share
what God has given you with others?

_____

_____

_____

_____

_____

_____

_____

_____

_____

_____

_____

_____

_____

_____

_____

_____

_____

_____

PART THREE:

JumpStart is the working piece
of my Doctor of Ministry Project.
One of the sections of my final paper was titled
THEOLOGICAL RATIONALE.

That is a fancy way to justify what I think
about what the Bible says about something.
If there is not a solid Scriptural foundation for something,
then we should not be doing it.

Exceptions are things like ice cream and airplanes.
There are not a lot of passages on jets and Coffee Hagen Dazs.
But I like them both.

If you are ready to dig a bit deeper
this Part of Mentor Training will give you my
Biblical foundations for JumpStart.

THE THEOLOGICAL RATIONALE
FOR JUMPSTART MENTOR TRAINING
Chapter Eighteen

Three Biblical assumptions reside at the core of this project. First, Scripture gives powerful models of people passing on their spiritual insights to other people. Second, Scripture is an essential component in the discipleship process. Third, disciples are part of the broader Body of Christ. Each of these three points undergirds an essential component of the JumpStart journey.

Person-to-Person Discipleship is an Essential Component of Spiritual Formation

Bill Hull is a church planter and lifelong advocate of disciple making. He gives an opening observation about the place of discipleship in the church and the role it plays in raising up spiritual leaders:

> Jesus believed in spiritual multiplication. He took the long view of what was necessary for a strong movement. The patient training of disciples is the only means unanimously endorsed by Scripture for building the Church. In contrast, we see in the twentieth century the shortcut, pragmatic approach. When churches try one crash program after another without strengthening the body of disciples, volumes of time and energy are wasted. If our ministries do not lead to the making of obedient fruit-bearing believers, then we have simply "fattened up" the church.[2]

Hull is embracing and applying the final words of Jesus as recorded in the gospel of Matthew. He is highlighting the importance of person-to-person contact:

> Jesus came and told his disciples, "I have been given all authority in heaven and on earth. Therefore, go and make disciples of all the nations, baptizing them in the name of the Father and the Son and the Holy Spirit. Teach these new disciples to obey all the commands I have given you. And be sure of this: I am with you always, even to the end of the age.[3]

This pattern of disciple making, also called mentoring, has deep roots in the Biblical record. This section will examine a mentoring relationship in the Pentateuch, the Prophets, and the New Testament. Discipleship did not begin with Jesus. He practiced it, and perfected it, but he did not begin it.

---

[2]Bill Hull, *Jesus Christ Disciple Maker* (Colorado Springs: Navpress, 1984), 38.
[3]Matthew 28:18-20 NLT

We know Moses as the giver of the Law of God. Moses went up the mountain to meet with God. However, Moses was not completely alone on this pivotal journey. "So Moses and his assistant Joshua set out, and Moses climbed up the mountain of God. Moses told the elders, 'Stay here and wait for us until we come back. Aaron and Hur are here with you. If anyone has a dispute while I am gone, consult with them.'"[4] God allowed Joshua to walk farther and closer, with Moses, than anyone else. Joshua's special relationship with Moses granted him a special access to God.

Joshua saw the relationship Moses had with God from a vantage point unlike anyone else's. "Whenever Moses went out to the Tent of Meeting, all the people would get up and stand in the entrances of their own tents. They would all watch Moses until he disappeared inside."[5] "Inside the Tent of Meeting, the LORD would speak to Moses face to face, as one speaks to a friend. Afterward Moses would return to the camp, but the young man who assisted him, Joshua son of Nun, would remain behind in the Tent of Meeting."[6] Joshua was serving and assisting Moses while Moses was speaking with God. The rest of the camp stood a safe distance away in the entrances to their tents while Joshua disappeared inside with Moses. In his capacity as assistant to Moses, Joshua saw and heard things that would one day prepare him to lead the nation.

Dr. William Mounce writes about the special role Moses had in the life of Joshua. He shows the relational, educational, encouraging, and modeling dimensions in the discipleship relationship between Moses and Joshua:

> He must have been a natural leader but his leadership potential was developed by studying under Moses and by learning from experience… Joshua studied under the master. He was Moses second in command, and aide… Joshua was with Moses on Sinai (Exod. 32:17), underwent religious experiences with Moses in the tent (33:11), and was personally ordained by Moses (Num. 27:18-23; Deut. 31:14-23). Notice too that Moses "encouraged" Joshua (Deut. 1:38).[7]

Joshua had the amazing privilege and responsibility of serving Moses for forty years. He saw the relationship Moses had with God. He watched as Moses led the people. He tasted the frustration of leadership when the nation rejected his good report regarding the Promised Land.[8] He learned the thrill of victory in battle.[9] It is no surprise "after the death of Moses the LORD's servant, the LORD spoke to Joshua son of Nun, Moses' assistant. He said, 'Moses my servant is dead. Therefore, the time has come for you to lead these

---

[4]Exodus 24:13-14 NLT
[5]Exodus 33:8 NLT
[6]Exodus 33:11 NLT
[7]William D. Mounce, *Profiles in Faith* (Ventura: Regal Books, 1984), 66-67.
[8]Numbers 16:13
[9]Exodus 17:13

people, the Israelites, across the Jordan River into the land I am giving them.'"[10] Joshua stepped into a role for which he had been fully prepared.

Thought:

If you are mentoring someone for a position of leadership in the church allow them to shadow you. If they are preparing to serve in a different capacity, then find a healthy believer who is currently doing that job, who will accept a shadow. Joshua was with Moses. He saw what he did, listened to his conversations, and shared his encounters with the Almighty. Joshua had the very best OJT possible. [On the Job Training.]

Elijah and Elisha provide another example of intimate relationship and the transference of spiritual authority. The responsibilities of his office had taken their toll upon Elijah. It was time for another man to arise and stand for God. God told Elijah to "anoint Elisha son of Shaphat from the town of Abel-meholah to replace you as my prophet."[11] Elisha accepted the call and "went with Elijah as his assistant."[12] If, as some have suggested, Elisha served Elijah from 860-850 BC, then there was a ten-year bond of service, and learning.

This tenure would underscore the intimacy seen in 2 Kings 2. The time has come for Elijah to return to heaven. Three times Elijah tells Elisha to "stay here." Three times Elisha responds with the passionate declaration, "As surely as the LORD lives and you yourself live, I will never leave you."[13] When the prophets from Bethel and Jericho ask Elisha if he knows God is preparing to take his master, he responds with an emphatic, "Of course I know."[14]

To those outside the master-servant bond, Elisha gives a curt, "Of course I know." To his master Elisha he gives the passionate promise, "As surely as the Lord lives and you yourself live, I will never leave you." As Elijah and Elisha continue their journey, "Fifty men from the group of prophets also went and watched from a distance as Elijah and Elisha stopped beside the Jordan River."[15] The fifty prophets watched from a distance, in much the same way as the children of Israel watched Moses and Joshua disappear into the Tent of Meeting. There is a holy separation between the mentor, the mentee, and the rest of the people.

There is evidence of ministry investment, authority transference, and a special relationship when "Elijah said to Elisha, 'Tell me what I can do for you before I am taken away.' And Elisha replied, 'Please let me inherit a double share of your spirit and become your successor.'"[16] The relationship and trust acquired over a long period of intimacy and

---

[10]Joshua 1:1-2 NLT
[11]1 Kings 19:16 NLT
[12]1 Kings 19:21 NLT
[13]2 Kings 2:2 NLT; 2 Kings 2:4 NLT; 2 Kings 2:6 NLT
[14]2 Kings 2:3 NLT; 2 Kings 2:5 NLT
[15]2 Kings 2:7 NLT
[16]2 Kings 2:9 NLT

service allows for such a request. The desire of Elisha is to be like Elijah and to do the things, which he saw him do. When God answers Elisha's request he manifests the profound combination of sorrow at the disappearance of his master and the willingness to pick up his mantle and follow his example.

Elisha stayed faithful to his promise and witnessed the moment when God came for Elijah. He cried out, 'My father! My father! I see the chariots and charioteers of Israel!' And as they disappeared, Elisha tore his clothes in distress. Elisha picked up Elijah's cloak, which had fallen when he was taken up. Then Elisha returned to the bank of the Jordan River. He struck the water with Elijah's cloak and cried out, 'Where is the LORD, the God of Elijah?' Then the river divided, and Elisha went across.[17] God confirmed the transference of spiritual authority and power from mentor to mentee.

In his form-critical commentary of II Kings, Burke Long highlights the separateness of Elijah and Elisha from the other prophets of Israel:

> From one point of view more talk means further delay in the progress of events. Yet, unlike the dialogues, which preceded it, this last exchange in this set-apart space offers the surprise that the departure of Elijah has also to do with the empowering of Elisha. As the Jordan marks divisions among the prophets, so this new information creates a kind of gnostic bond between Elijah and Elisha. With the reader, they now share a knowledge that is denied those prophets left behind at the thresholding river.[18]

Jesus Christ is the Christian's ultimate example of disciple making. The Mount of Transfiguration offers what is arguably the greatest theophany of the New Testament. The passage highlights Moses as the giver of the Law, and Elijah as one of the greatest power prophets. While this is certainly the case, it is also a great gathering of mentors. Moses, Elijah, and Jesus do not only represent the Law, the prophets, and the new covenant but they also surely connect the millennium old tradition of mentoring, disciple making, and relationship-based leader training.

What Moses and Elijah did in the lives of Joshua and Elisha are precursors to what Jesus Christ did with Peter, James, and John. Jesus Christ gave the vision and the method behind discipleship when he said, "Follow Me, and I will make you fishers of men."[19] There is no making without following. Jesus extended his invitation to twelve men. Within the twelve, three received special access. Jesus allowed Peter, James, and John to see the gathering of

---

[17] 2 Kings 2:12-14 NLT

[18] *2 Kings*, The Forms of the Old Testament Literature, Burke O. Long, volume 10, (Grand Rapids: Wm. B. Eerdmans Publishing Co., 1991), 26.

[19] Matthew 4:19 NASB

mentors on the Mount of Transfiguration while the rest of the disciples waited in the valley below.[20] I wonder if the three truly understood the uniqueness of their experience.

When Jesus, and the disciples, were on their way to the home of Jairus to attend his sick daughter, they received the news his daughter had died. As the men were giving Jairus the news, "Jesus overheard them and said to Jairus, 'Don't be afraid. Just have faith.' Then Jesus stopped the crowd and wouldn't let anyone go with him except Peter, James, and John (the brother of James)."[21] Jesus is preparing to bless a brokenhearted family with the greatest of miracles. He is going to give them back their daughter. Jesus only allows his three most trusted disciples, Peter, James, and John, to partake in the experience.

On the final night of his life, Jesus led his eleven faithful disciples to the Garden of Gethsemane. This was His time to connect with the Father and confirm that He was travelling the only path possible: "They went to the olive grove called Gethsemane, and Jesus said, 'Sit here while I go and pray.' He took Peter, James, and John with him, and He became deeply troubled and distressed."[22] Jesus allowed Peter, James, and John to see the depth of His emotions. He allowed these three intimate followers to see His distress.

Peter, James, and John enjoyed an access the other nine disciples did not seem to have. Jesus allowed them to hear God on the mountain. They watched Jesus minister at the home of Jairus. They enjoyed a closer access to the pain and trial of Christ in the Garden of Gethsemane. It is not surprising that John was known as the disciple whom Jesus loved and was granted eyes to see the glorified Christ.[23] It is not surprising that Peter preached the tide-turning sermon on the day the church was born.[24] It is not surprising that when King Herod began his persecution of the church, it started with one of the key leaders. "About that time King Herod Agrippa began to persecute some believers in the church. He had the apostle James (John's brother) killed with a sword.[25] The Apostle Paul makes a telling declaration regarding the special mentees of Jesus. He writes "James, Peter, and John, who were known as pillars of the church, recognized the gift God had given me." Paul, who never cited any source save Christ for the legitimacy of his ministry, acknowledges the special position that Peter, James, and John held in the early church.[26] Their special positions in the early church was a direct result of the special place they occupied in the relational training program of Jesus Christ.

---

[20]Matthew 17
[21]Mark 5:36-37 NLT
[22]Mark 14:32-33 NLT
[23]Revelation 1:12-13
[24]Acts 2:14
[25] Acts 12:1-2 NLT
[26] Galatians 2:9 NLT

The Study of Scripture is an Essential Component in the Equipping of Disciples

The previous section examined the call Christ gave to make disciples. In this section, an examination of the place of the Scriptures in that process will follow. Jesus told the people who believed in him, "You are truly my disciples if you remain faithful to my teachings."[27] He concluded his earthly ministry with a clear call to implement the training of disciples. He said, "Teach these new disciples to obey all the commands I have given you."[28]

The Apostle Paul puts the words and example of Jesus into practice in the book of Second Timothy. Paul is mentoring Timothy, his spiritual son in the Christian faith in the whys and ways of ministry.[29]

The call to be a workman who is not ashamed still beckons through this verse: "Study to shew thyself approved unto God, a workman that needeth not to be ashamed, rightly dividing the word of truth."[30] Kenneth Wuest gives an expanded translation and explanation of these ancient words. The following paragraph conveys his quotes and translations.

The Apostle Paul is challenging his mentee, young Timothy, to *spoudazo*. He wants him to study, "to make haste, to exert one's self, endeavor, and give diligence."[31] Paul wants him to *paristemi,* to shew, to present, "to show, the quality which the person or thing exhibits."[32] He wants Timothy to be *dokimos* for God. He wants him "put to the test for the purpose of approving, and finding that the person or thing meets the specifications laid down, to put one's approval upon that person or thing."[33] Paul wants Timothy approved as a workman of God. "A workman approved is a workman who has been put to the test, and meeting the specifications, has won the approval of the one who has subjected him to the test."[34] This approved workman of God is one who can *orthotomeo*. He is one who can "cut it straight."[35] Wuest quotes Vincent regarding the intent of the workman. "The thought is that the minister of the gospel is to present the truth rightly, not abridging it, not handling it as a charlatan, not making it a matter of wordy strife, but treating it honestly and fully,

---

[27]John 8:31 NLT

[28]Matthew 28:20

[29]Personal note: When I was a new believer in Christ, John Gossett, a deacon in the Church of Christ had me memorize 2 Timothy 2:15 in the King James Version.
I have spent the past thirty-six years reflecting upon what it means to shew and divide.

[30]2 Timothy 2:15 KJV

[31] Kenneth S. Wuest, *Wuest's Word Studies*
(Grand Rapids: Wm. B. Eerdmans Publishing Company, 1952), 134-135.

[32]Wuest, 134-135.

[33]Wuest, 134-135.

[34]Wuest, 134-135.

[35]Wuest, 134-135.

in a straightforward manner."[36] Wuest helps us see the intention of the Apostle Paul, regarding the written word of God. The disciple who would serve Christ accurately and faithfully must first invest time in study to assure that when he or she speaks, he or she is treating the word of God like the tentmaker's cloth, and cutting it straight.

Pastor and author John McArthur confirms Wuest's challenge to handle the Word of God accurately and faithfully. He builds upon Vincent's metaphor of tent making.

> The mark of a faithful teacher or preacher [or mentor] is his handling accurately the word of truth. Handling accurately translates a participle of *orthotomeo*, which means literally to cut straight. It was used of a mason setting a straight line, of a farmer plowing a straight furrow, of a mason setting a straight line of bricks, or of workmen building a straight road. Metaphorically, it was used of carefully performing any task. Because Paul was a tentmaker by trade (Acts 18:3), he may have had in mind the careful, straight cutting and sewing of the many pieces of leather or cloth necessary to make a tent.[37]

The Apostle goes on to give his mentee a progression for how the word can work in the development of a disciple. "All Scripture is inspired by God and is useful to teach us what is true and to make us realize what is wrong in our lives. It corrects us when we are wrong and teaches us to do what is right. God uses it to prepare and equip his people to do every good work."[38]

The God-breathed Scriptures begin by teaching what is true. When mortals attempt to align their lives with divine truth, they reveal the disparity between sinful humanity and holy divinity. This intersection is a great moment of decision for the aspiring disciple. When the Word of God begins to conflict with lives, believers have a choice. They may pursue a self-directed journey or repent and submit to God's Word and will. A willingness to abide in the process of correction opens the door to the realm of learning where the Word of God teaches what is right. Embracing truth, acknowledging wrong, accepting correction, and learning to do right puts the disciple of Jesus Christ on the path to service and the doing of good works.

When mentor and mentee meet to open the Scriptures, they are not alone. JumpStart teaches the participants to invite the Holy Spirit to come and be the teacher, leader, and guide who directs each conversation in the direction it needs to go. Scott Duval and Daniel Hays connect the work of the Holy Spirit on both sides of the text. The Holy Spirit is breathing the text into being, and He is present as teacher and guide to direct the seeker.

---

[36]Wuest, 134-135.
[37]John MacArthur, *2 Timothy,* in The MacArthur New Testament Commentary, (Chicago: Moody Press, 1995), 76.
[38]2 Timothy 3:16-17 NLT

The term *inspiration* refers to the Holy Spirit's work in the lives of the human authors of Scripture with the result that they wrote what God wanted to communicate (i.e., the Word of God). In 2 Timothy 3:16-17 the apostle Paul says that "all Scripture is *God-breathed* [sometimes translated *inspired*] and is useful for teaching, rebuking, correcting and training in righteousness, so that the servant of God may be thoroughly equipped for every good work." The Spirit of God has breathed the character of God into the Scriptures. The Greek word for "inspired" (*theopneustos*) is even related to the Greek word for "spirit" *(pneuma)*. The Bible has the power and authority to shape our lives because it comes from God himself.

We hold to the authority of the Scriptures because they are inspired ("God-breathed"). Paul's statement in II Timothy also reminds us that the Spirit and the Scriptures go together-the Word of God originated from the Spirit of God. The Spirit's work of inspiration is finished, but his work of bringing believers to understand and receive the truth of Scripture continues. Theologians use the term *illumination* to refer to this ongoing work of the Spirit. On the night before he was crucified, Jesus promised his followers that the Holy Spirit would guide them into all truth:[39]

As mentor and mentee open their hearts, minds, spirits, and lives to the teaching of the Scriptures, they can trust the promise of Christ to send them a teacher. In the mentoring guide for JumpStart, there is ongoing exhortation toward spiritual listening for what God is saying and doing during the meeting times. Systematic theologian Wayne Grudem describes this work of the Holy Spirit in the life of the student of Scripture:

> Our ultimate conviction that the words of the Bible are God's words comes only when the Holy Spirit speaks in and through the words of the Bible to our hearts and gives us an inner assurance that these are the words of our Creator speaking to us... Apart from the work of the Spirit of God, a person will not receive spiritual truths and in particular will not receive or accept the truth that the words of Scripture are in fact the words of God.[40]

Just as discipleship and mentoring have roots in the Old Testament, so do these principles of Scripture-based leader preparation. Ezra, the prophetic teacher, followed Paul's pattern almost five-hundred years before the Apostle Paul taught it to Timothy. The text reads, "...The gracious hand of his God was on him [Ezra]. This was because Ezra had determined to study and obey the Law of the LORD and to teach those decrees and regulations to the people of Israel."[41] Ezra followed the same pattern, which God gave to Joshua. "Study this Book of Instruction continually. Meditate on it day and night, so you will be sure to obey

---

[39] J. Scott Duvall, and J. Daniel Hays, *Grasping God's Word* (Grand Rapids: Zondervan, 2012), 226.
[40] Wayne Grudem, *Systematic Theology* (Leister, England: Inter-Varsity Press, 1994), 77.
[41] Ezra 7:9-10 NLT

everything written in it. Only then, will you prosper and succeed in all you do."[42] Charles Wilson affirms this pattern in the life of Ezra, calling him the "ideal Jewish scribe, dedicated to a threefold task; seeking to know the law, striving to obey it, and teaching it to others."[43]

One hundred years ago, the great preacher H. A. Ironside described this process at work within Ezra.

> Not a mere intellectual student of the word of God, nor one teaching others what had not gripped his own heart and controlled his ways, was Ezra. He had begun by earnestly preparing his own heart to seek the law of the Lord. The preparation of the heart in man is of the Lord. This Ezra recognized. So it is not said that he prepared his head-but his heart. His inmost being was brought under the sway of the truth of God. His affections were controlled by the Scriptures. He might have said with Jeremiah; "Thy words were found, and I did eat them; and thy word was unto me the joy and rejoicing of my heart." He was personally right with God, and so was prepared to help set others right. Then there was more than inward preparation. Having learned the mind and will of God, he undertook to do it. He did not preach truth he was not living.[44]

The study, acceptance, apprehension, internalization, and obedience to the Word of God is essential in the process of disciple making. JumpStart proposes to lead a seeker, or a growing believer, into a deeper interaction with God's Word, through the loving partnership of a man or woman who has himself or herself committed to study, internalize, and obey the word of God.

In his book, *The Wholehearted Church Planter,* professor, mentor, and church planter Allan Karr speaks of his Christian heritage. He testifies to the essential role of Scripture in becoming and remaining a "wholehearted" servant of God. "Being and remaining wholehearted involves knowing passages of Scripture, learning new passages and principles from Scripture, and listening to God through Scripture regularly. These daily practices remind me of what is already true and prove to be key to being and living the life Scripture reveals."[45]

---

[42] Joshua 1:8 NLT

[43] Charles R. Wilson, *Joshua-Esther,* Wesleyan Bible Commentary, ed. Charles W. Carter, vol. 1 (Grand Rapids: William B. Eerdmans Publishing Company, 1967), 447.

[44] H. A. Ironside, *Notes on Ezra, Nehemiah, and Esther* (New York: Loizeaux Brothers, 1913), 65-66.

[45] Allan Karr and Linda Bergquist, *The Wholehearted Church Planter* (St. Louis: Chalice Press, 2013), 19.

Disciples are Members of the Broader Body of Christ

American films portray heroes such as Tarzan, Superman, Roy Rodgers, and the Lone Ranger. Although Jane, Lois Lane, Dale Evans, and Tonto existed, they did not function as the driving force in the relationship. In American films, characters portrayed by Humphrey Bogart, John Wayne, Clint Eastwood, Arnold Schwarzenegger, Sylvester Stallone, and Bruce Willis portrayed the same rugged individualism. In the current reprise of the classic *Star Trek* franchise Captain Kirk is the clear leader while Spock, though higher up the intellectual scale, consistently follows the strong willed leader.

In his book, *The Church that Multiplies*, Dr. Joel Comiskey addresses this unique milieu of North American culture. Joel has studied the cell church both nationally and internationally. It is significant that in this book, he articulates the unique challenges and sociology of the Christian church in America. He writes, "North American culture in general focuses on the individual as opposed to the group. Each person is encouraged to think and act individually."[46] Comiskey cites the American propensity toward cultural individualism as a possible source of hindrance to the healthy development of cell churches in the North American context.[47] JumpStart came into being within the context of a cell church model of ministry. Because disciples function within the framework of Life Groups it is essential that the disciple's connection to the larger Body of Christ be clearly understood.

Classical evangelism in the American context often includes some form of invitation to receive Jesus Christ as personal Lord and Savior. While this connects with the teaching of Jesus to follow him, it falls woefully short of the fullness which life in the Body of Christ offers. The call to "follow me" resonates with the individual spirit of Americans. The call to belong is oftentimes a much greater challenge. Traditional American culture does not readily embrace concepts such as mutual submission and interpersonal accountability. In his work, which examines *Why Men Hate Church,* David Murrow makes a troubling observation about men and their thinking in regards to relationships. "A lot of guys have messed up every relationship they've ever had, so they associate the word with hurt, misunderstanding, and pain. In a man's mind, relationships are something men have with women, not with other men. A man has to overcome a truckload of fear and suspicion to have a relationship with another man."[48]

Discover the opposite of American individualism in the words of the Apostle Paul to the church in Rome where he declares, "We are many parts of one body, and we all belong to

---

[46]Joel Comiskey, *The Church That Multiplies* (Moreno Valley: CCS Publishing, 2007), 39.

[47]Comiskey, The Church that Multiplies, 40.

[48]David Murrow, *Why Men Hate Going to Church* (Nashville: Thomas Nelson, 2005), 223.

each other."[49] Biblical belonging occurs in authentic community. Dr. Ralph W. Neighbour, Jr. writes,

> "Because community can occur most completely only in small groups, a cell group, numbering less than 15 people, is all important. Essential elements of community include interpersonal commitments and a sense of belonging. Community takes place when there is a shared life, allowing common goals and commitments to develop between all of its members."[50]

Shared life is essential because "all have been baptized into one body by one Spirit."[51] Howard A. Snyder challenges the idea of Christian individualism and instead advocates intimate relationships within the Body of Christ.

> Today the church needs to rediscover what the early Christians found: That small group meetings are something essential to Christian experience and growth. That the success of a church function is not measured by body count. That without the small group the church in urban society simply does not experience one of the most basic essentials of the gospel-true, rich deep Christian soul-fellowship, or *koinonia.*[52]

Snyder is pointing to the *koinonia* of the early church as seen in Acts 2:42 where, "All the believers devoted themselves to the apostles teaching, and to fellowship, and to sharing in meals (including the Lord's Supper), and to prayer."[53] C. Peter Wagner captures the essence of this dynamic of following Christ and living in the body. "While they were growing in their vertical relationship to God, the new believers were also growing in their horizontal relationship to each other in Christian fellowship."[54] As the Apostle Paul teaches us, "All of you together are Christ's body, and each of you is a part of it."[55]

The approach the church takes toward mentoring and leader training must support and demonstrate this commitment to relationships. Rowland Forman, Jeff Jones, and Bruce Miller ask and answer a rhetorical question, which speaks to this context for leader training.

> If the church is at its core a closely-knit community of love, a less-than-perfect community of forgiven sinners, what does this mean for leadership development? We need leaders who embody what the church is. We need leaders who are

---

[49]Romans 12:5 NLT
[50]Neighbour, Where do we go From Here? 113.
[51]1 Corinthians 12:13 NLT
[52]Howard A. Snyder, *The problem of Wineskins*
(Downers Grove: Intervarsity Press, 1975), 140.
[53]Acts 2:42 NLT
[54]C. Peter Wagner, *Spreading the Fire* (Ventura: Regal Books, 1994), 104.
[55]1 Corinthians 12:27 NLT

passionate about modeling community and who are committed to developing other leaders in the context of community.[56]

These theological presuppositions are at the philosophical center of training mentors to utilize JumpStart. They follow the pattern of person-to-person leader training/mentoring. Each session of JumpStart has its foundation in the written Word of God. Finally, the sessions invite each participant to take his or her rightful place within the Body of Christ.

Conclusion:

Thank you for taking the time to read through this last section. Hopefully, it confirmed for you that JumpStart stands on solid Biblical footing. Sadly, the church tends to acknowledge the Biblical importance of discipleship, without doing it. I think there are two major problems.

First, we do not know how. I suspect that many, if not most believers, are timid about presenting themselves as a mentor for another. It sounds arrogant and presumptuous. Andy Stanley, Lead Pastor of NorthPoint Atlanta shared a liberating thought at the Catalyst Conference a few years ago. He said, "You are not responsible to fill somebody else's cup. You are simply called to empty your own cup." How liberating is that? I do not need to know everything. All I need do is share what God has given me with those God brings me. I can do that, and so can you.

Second, it is slow. We want quick easy results. Churches want growth. They want excitement. Discipleship is not necessarily quick or exciting. Either are the roots of a Redwood. Yet, without the interconnected network of roots Redwood trees would fall over in the first big wind. The numerical potential of discipleship is well known. For old times' sake, let's close with it! Imagine if your mentors multiplied every six months. Let's begin with five faithful mentors and run it out a few years. What could this do in your church, chapel, or ministry setting? It is slow. But it is powerful, Biblical, and explosive! And what happens if you find that 30, 60, 100-fold person, and disciple them?

5	10	20	40	80
160	320	640	1,280	2,560
5,120	10,240	20,480	40,960	

---

[56]Rowland Forman, Jeff Jones, and Bruce Miller, *The Leadership Baton*
(Grand Rapids: Zondervan, 2004), 92.

Hello artist friends.
Any last images about the place of discipleship in today's world?

EPILOGUE

I do not guide my life by numbers. Having said that, there are Biblical numbers and patterns with deep significance. I was baptized in October, married in October, installed as pastor of NorthPoint in October, and presented JumpStart outside the walls of NorthPoint for the first time in October. I am writing this in October of 2016. Go figure!

I became a Christian in 1977. My last day as Lead Pastor of NorthPoint is 1/1/17. Launching into JumpStart Mentor Training coincides with my forty-year anniversary as a Christ Follower. The number forty often accompanies a special event or the end of a season of life.

Ralph W. Neighbour, Jr. told me to write JumpStart while we were in Waco, TX in 2009. At the time, I was doing a forty day fast. I returned from Waco in July of 2009. I have often wondered what that fast impacted because none of the things I was praying about ended up the way I planned. Just the other night it hit me. JumpStart published in July of 2016, seven years to the month after it began. So, a journey I began with a forty day fast took seven years to complete. Seven is the Biblical number of completion.

A forty day fast, seven years of work, and forty years of preparation. I could also push it and say if you multiplied the perfect number three times the number of completion seven you come up with the 21 years I have pastored NorthPoint. Like I said, I do not guide my life by numbers, but they sure can be interesting.

I share these random thoughts with you because it is time for me to launch out and see what God wants to do with JumpStart. I covet your prayers for me as I joyfully pray for you. God can break any chain and bring light into any depth of darkness. His Word and kingdom truly are mustard seeds. If you do your best to plow, plant, water, and tend I believe He will do the miraculous work of raisin up disciple making mentors in your ministry. They will multiply your ability to reach, minister, and train beyond anything you have ever seen.

And now may the God of Glory fill you with grace, health, power, peace, faith, and persistence for the journey He has called you to. May souls be saved, believers trained, and leaders released up to do their Masters business. May God open doors that no man can shut and shut doors that no man can open. May God given signs and wonders follow you and your ministry all the days of your life. May you be that 100-fold Christ follower!

In the name of the Father,
and the Son,
and the Holy Ghost.
        AMEN!

ABOUT THE AUTHOR:

Dr. Paul M. Reinhard was born at Ft. Sill, OK in 1955. His family soon returned to Southern California where he grew up and spent his youth. He graduated from Glendale High in 1973 and joined the U.S. Army on April 1, 1974. APRIL FOOLS!

He spent the next four years training and serving. He was on A-732 in Seventh Special Forces Group, and A-595 in Fifth Special Forces Group. Paul graduated from High Altitude Low Opening Parachute School (HALO) and Special Forces Under Water Operations (SFUWO). His team attended Jungle School in Panama, mountain operations in Puerto Rico, and Winter Warfare training in Alaska during January. During his last season of service his team worked and trained with a SADM (Strategic Atomic Demolition Munition.) This part of his training was only recently declassified by the U.S. Army.

While Paul held a Nuclear level security clearance by day he and his friends were devout "party animals" by night. In the summer of 1977 Paul's crazy lifestyle brought him to the point of decision. Through a multitude of "chance" encounters and events the Lord Jesus called Paul out of his sinful lifestyle and into the church.

In 1978 Paul was honorably discharged from the Army and returned to Glendale, CA. He met and married Karen Louise Maddux. He was attending L.I.F.E. Bible college when they learned Karen was pregnant with their first child. Paul needed a job so he applied, and was accepted, to the Glendale Police Department. Chris was born July 5, 1980 just days before Paul graduated from the Los Angeles Sheriff's Academy, Class 200.

While Glendale PD paid the bills Paul's heart and call where toward the ministry. Over the next few years Paul sold cars, ran a gardening route, and ultimately graduated from Azusa Pacific University with a B.A. in Biblical Literature. Daughter Jennifer was born July 20th, 1983 while Paul was still a student. He graduated in 1985.

The family began youth ministry at Sunland Baptist Church. Paul continued to study at Fuller Seminary. In 1988 the family moved to Fresno and Paul continued to study at California Theological Seminary by night. He worked at Power Burst as the Director of Special Events by day. In 1992 the family packed it up and moved to Woodstown, N.J. Paul was the part time Youth Pastor at First Baptist Church and a full time student at Eastern Baptist Theological Seminary, now Palmer Seminary. Paul graduated in 1994. In 1995 Paul accepted the call to Calvary Baptist Church in San Bernardino, CA where he pastored for twenty-one years.

Paul and Karen spent twenty-one years leading the church through a name change to NorthPoint, multimillion dollar arson fire, bankrupt insurance company, rebuild, and debt survival. They persisted in guiding a traditional Baptist church through changes in worship, constitution, and membership. Today the church is unified, growing, and pursuing God's will for her future under the excellent leadership of their son Chris!

In 2008 Paul began the Doctor of Ministry program at Golden Gate Theological Seminary, now Gateway. He had the privilege of being in the Cell Church cohort led by Dr. Ralph Neighbour, Jr. Over the past eight years God has tightened Paul's focus. Paul embraces large groups and loves Life Groups. However, he believes it is the one-on-one experience which transforms lives, shapes character, and prepares leaders.

Paul and Karen love doing life with their children Christopher and Jennifer, their spouses Shannon and Jeremy, and their six grandchildren Ashlee, Zoe, Hannah, Luke, Noah, and Busy Lizzy.

At sixty-one years of age Paul is feeling very blessed, alive, and curious about the next forty years! If Paul can serve you, your church, chapel, or ministry by speaking, dreaming, coaching, mentoring, or praying please reach out and connect.

CALL OR TEXT:
909-855-9695

EMAIL:
PaulMReinhard@Gmail.Com

PRAYERS AND NOTES:

PRAYERS AND NOTES:

PRAYERS AND NOTES:

Made in the USA
Middletown, DE
18 November 2016